To Wayne,

Best Wishes from

a very greatful city

Your Friend

Mayor Richard Neal

May 23, 1985

This book
is
dedicated to
the
City of Springfield
on its
350th Anniversary

Nationally known engraver Thomas Chubbock designed and executed this version of the Springfield City Seal in 1853. The seal shows the seventeenth-century Pynchon "mansion house" (lower right) and the nineteenth-century technological and industrial developments that made Springfield a thriving city: the Armory arsenal (top), the railroad terminal (below the arsenal), and the Connecticut River with steamboat and factories (left side). Courtesy of the mayor's office, city of Springfield

Design by Joan Croyder

THE DONNING COMPANY/PUBLISHERS
NORFOLK/VIRGINIA BEACH

Springfield—350 Years
A PICTORIAL HISTORY

By Donald J. D'Amato

The Donning Company/Publishers
5659 Virginia Beach Boulevard
Norfolk, Virginia 23502

Library of Congress Cataloging-in-Publication Data

D'Amato, Donald J., 1943-
    Springfield---350 years.
    Bibliography: p.
    Includes index.
    1. Springfield (Mass.)---Description---Views.
2. Springfield (Mass.)---History---Pictorial works. I. Title.
II. Springfield---Three hundred fifty years.
F74.S8143D36   1985   974.4'26   85-25211
ISBN 0-89865-441-6

Printed in the United States of America

CONTENTS

"The Birth of Springfield" Painting by J. J. La Valley

INTRODUCTION

MAYOR RICHARD E. NEAL

City of Springfield
36 Court Street
Springfield, Ma 01103
Tel.(413) 787-6100

Dr. Donald J. D'Amato has assembled four essays and almost 400 photographs that detail the rich history of Springfield, and the many changes the city has gone through-from its beginning as a fur trading post on the banks of the Connecticut River-to its position as one of the leading and most vital cities of New England. Here are photographs that trace the development of Springfield's neighborhoods, businesses, industries, buildings, streets and, most importantly, its people.

Richard E. Neal

MILES·MORGAN
AN·EARLY·SETTLER·OF
SPRINGFIELD·DIED·DAY
ERECTED·IN·1882·BY·ONE
OF·HIS·DESCENDANTS·OF
THE·FIFTH·GENERATION

PREFACE

The people of Springfield are surrounded by history. Preceded by fourteen generations of citizens, present-day residents are a part of history and history is a part of them. There are no streets, no neighborhoods, no buildings, no parks which do not reflect these prior generations' human experiences. The people of Springfield should be proud of their heritage, their inheritance, their city.

The writing of this history would not have been possible without the help of the following people: Joseph Carvallio III, supervisor, Genealogy and Local History Room of the Springfield City Library, and his assistants: Arline S. Morton, Edmond Lonergan, and Guy McLain, who searched the Local History Room's files and shelves for requested materials. Discussions with Ed helped to keep the city's architectural history in perspective. Andrew B. Searle of Springfield Central provided information and photographs concerning downtown redevelopment.

I would also like to thank Mayor Richard E. Neal for his support and encouragement, Carol P. Petell for her excellent artwork, and Stanislaus J. Skarzynski for his photography work. I would like to especially thank Richard C. Garvey, editor of the *Springfield Daily News* and well-known local historian, for proofreading the final copy of the text. His suggestions improved the accuracy and the readability of the book. I would also like to thank Attorney Leonard R. Skvirsky—avid collector of the city memorabilia and one of the first businessmen to revitalize a downtown building, demonstrating his faith in the city's future—for his enthusiasm about and support of this book. For the many unnamed others who provided photographs and information, thank you. A special thanks goes to my wife, Marlene—my editor and my typist—who has always understood and supported my love of local history.

The Seventeenth Century:
A Village In The Wilderness

Chapter One

In July 1636 William Pynchon and seven other men purchased land on both sides of the Connecticut River. In that same year he and the others established a settlement, Agawam Plantation, on the east side of the river at the present site of Springfield, Massachusetts. In 1636 the settlement was located on an island which ran from about the location of Valle's Steak House in the North End to the present York Street in the South End. The island was about one mile wide with a hill of varying heights running the length of its spine.

The island was really a spit of not-very-fertile sand with the Connecticut River to the west and marsh, pond, and swamp to the north, east, and south. Directly to the east and parallel to the island was the Hassocky Marsh, a remnant of an older Connecticut River channel. The marsh was so named because large tufts of grass, once used to stuff footstools, grew there. Beyond the marsh, further to the east, was a pine barren dotted with brooks, ponds, and swampland. At the site of the present Winchester Square were two large ponds together known as Goose Pond; a large swamp was located where Blunt Park is today. Barrens, swamps, and beaver ponds alternated to the Wilbraham hills beyond present-day Sixteen Acres; the Forest Park neighborhood was full of scrub pine, sand, more beaver ponds, and ravines running east-west; and East Springfield was hilly woodland interspersed with flat meadow. The Springfield area had little forest, and the soil generally became less fertile, less suitable for farming, as one traveled east or west of the Connecticut River.

Agawam Plantation was carefully designed. The town lots, individual grants of land, were laid out on the west side of present-day Main Street. The east side was uninhabitable because of the marsh. Only forty house lots were laid out because Pynchon and the men who agreed to settle the plantation wanted to limit the settlement to forty but no more than fifty families. House lots averaged about four acres. Pynchon received the largest portion of land because the settlement was his idea, and he paid the local Indians about half the purchase price for the new town's land. Each of the lots ran to the river and was to be fenced by order of the town. All lot owners received a strip of land as wide as their house lot in and beyond the Hassocky Marsh. This plot was a wood lot, necessary to provide firewood for each household. Each settler also received a plot of land on the west side of the river for raising corn, since the most fertile land in the area was there.

Construction of buildings was slow. A lot was set aside for a town minister, but a house was not built until 1639. A meetinghouse, where religious services and town meetings were held, was not built until 1645. It stood on the southeast corner of present-day Court Square, facing present-day Elm Street.

Elm Street, a sixteen-foot-wide dirt lane known as the "lane to the middle landing," ran to a Pynchon-owned wharf on the river. Later the lane was called "the way to the training place" because the local militia drilled on a nearby field, now also part of Court Square. Until 1645 religious services and government-related meetings were held in Pynchon's house, built near the corner of present-day Fort and Main streets.

Early settlers found a ledge of sandstone near present-day Benton Street next to Massachusetts Mutual. The ledge was important because it provided stone for house foundations and chimneys. Stone pit road or the "middle causeway," now State Street, therefore developed as a town road, making the ledge accessible to early builders. The middle causeway, originally built in 1648, was a corduroy road. The roadway, the only land passage off the plantation, was constructed of logs pressed into the muck of the marsh. Today the remains of the corduroy road can be found about six feet beneath State Street next to the Civic Center.

The Connecticut River provided the fastest, most convenient way to travel, since few roads existed. The Pynchon family used the river as a highway, shipping out beaver and other animal pelts and produce while shipping in goods to trade with the Indians or to sell in William Pynchon's trade house located at the foot of present-day Longhill Street. The river was the only convenient way to reach a corn mill that John Pynchon, William's son, built and operated on the Mill River. Eventually a bridge was built across the Mill River, and a second corduroy road, the "lower causeway," was built. This second causeway crossed the marsh at the south end of town, leading to the present Locust Street area which, at that time, flooded regularly every spring. By 1643 Main Street extended south beyond the present York Street, angling westward toward the Connecticut River as it does today.

A third corduroy road, the "upper causeway," was built across the northern section of the Hassocky Marsh and is now Carew Street. By 1710 the upper and middle causeways were connected by a narrow path, the present Chestnut Street. Throughout the seventeenth and the first half of the eighteenth centuries, these narrow dirt paths—bordered by marsh, swamp, or stream and subject to seasonal flooding—were the principal streets of early Springfield.

The area of settlement contained a number of streams. The source of Garden Brook was the ponds at present-day Winchester Square. The brook followed a circuitous route, reflecting the hilly and ravine-filled nature of the city's early geography. It flowed down to the present Spring Street, turned south, then north near the corner of Chestnut and Worthington streets, flowed north around the Round Hill, once located to the north of the Coca-Cola plant on West Street and now the site of a highway interchange, and finally west and into the river. A second brook ran from a swampy ravine known as Skunk's Misery, the present site of Commerce High School. The swamp was so named because of the foul odors which rose from it. Skunk's Misery Brook flowed down to Main Street along the present street lines of High, Temple, and Stockbridge. At Main Street it turned south and flowed into the Connecticut River below York Street.

Skunk's Misery Swamp ran the length of High Street and was dotted with quicksand bogs. In the early nineteenth century difficult children were told to "go play in the swamp." A number of children actually drowned in the brook or were lost in the bogs. When Classical High School was built, a quicksand bog on Temple Street had to be filled with stone trucked to the site by horse-drawn wagons before a firm building foundation could be laid.

Eventually the Garden and Skunk's Misery brooks were connected by a man-made ditch. Each seventeenth-century lot owner was required by law to dig a ditch the width of his property on the east side of Main Street. The object of this labor was to provide a drainage ditch for the Hassocky Marsh. The completed trench paralleled the length of Main Street from State Street to the Garden Brook. Depending upon the water level, this man-made brook—called the Town Brook—flowed either north or south. It was the town's water supply for almost 200 years. Gradually the marsh drained into the Town Brook and became a meadow used to pasture animals. Damp and spongy, it was unsuitable for building.

The site William Pynchon chose for Agawam Plantation was unappealing. The land was infertile or considered unimprovable. The topography was rugged. Families who came to Springfield in those days were looking for good farmland, so they settled elsewhere. During the early years of settlement, the little village did not grow as a farming community. It did, however, develop as a trading post—the initial reason for its founding.

William Pynchon, a Puritan, was born in 1590 in Springfield, England—now a suburb of London. In 1629 when the English Puritans were granted the right to settle in the New World by the king of England, Pynchon was the group's treasurer. It was his responsibility to gather the military supplies required by the Massachusetts Bay Colony.

Little is known of Pynchon's early life. Evidence suggests that he was a gentleman farmer of some wealth. He was also literate, but it is not known where he was educated. Since he is such a shadowy figure, his reasons for migrating to North America can only be guessed. Because he was a Puritan, he may have migrated for the sake of religious freedom. The Puritans were unhappy members of the Church of England who considered the religious practices of that church too Catholic. Therefore, they migrated across 3,000 miles of ocean to escape the religious practices and influences they thought dangerous to salvation. In the wilderness of the New World they would be able to "purify" their own brand of Protestantism and prepare for the Day of Judgment and for salvation. Personal wealth may also have been a motivation to cross the ocean. To the Puritans, religion and personal wealth were linked. If a man were truly one of God's chosen people—predestined for Heaven—financial success could be the earthly evidence of eventual salvation.

Whatever his beliefs and motivations, soon after arriving in the Bay Colony, Pynchon became active in the fur trade. In 1630 he settled at Roxbury, now part of Boston. At least one ship financed by Pynchon, a shallop, sailed up and down the coast trading for furs with both English settlers and Indians. The venture, however, was not successful. Competition was too intense and the availability in the Boston area of quality pelts, especially beaver, was declining. In 1632, to add to his difficulties, Pynchon's trade ship ran aground and was lost, though crew and cargo were saved. As the supply of beaver pelts became scarce, furs were purchased from Indians who journeyed to Boston from the western wilderness of present-day Massachusetts and the Connecticut Valley.

Pynchon became interested in the valley. He may have heard stories from explorer John Oldham of the valley's riches in fur-bearing animals, good soil, and friendly Indians. Oldham and several other frontiersmen had walked overland from Boston to the Connecticut Valley and had returned with furs, seed corn, hemp, and white lead. Although the Indians were friendly, the English were fearful. There were purportedly 5,000 Indian warriors in the valley north of Hartford, a danger to the survival of any town newly settled in that area. In 1633 the Indians of the valley suffered an epidemic, most likely smallpox, and many died. One source, perhaps a fragment of a letter written by a Dutch trader speaks of more than 900 Indian deaths in an area populated by about 1,000 people. The trader may have been referring to the Indians of the Springfield area.

In the fall of 1635 Pynchon and five other men sailed up the Connecticut River. Pynchon was interested in establishing a permanent settlement far upriver, a settlement which would intercept the Indian fur trade before it reached Boston. He chose a site for a trading post on the west side of the Connecticut River in present-day Agawam. The location was excellent. The woods and meadows were full of bear, fox, moose, fruits and berries, and well-stocked beaver ponds, therefore providing both food and animal pelts. The surrounding rivers—the Agawam, now known as the Westfield River, the Connecticut, the Chicopee—were full of shad, salmon, and other fish. These would provide food as well as ease of transportation, since heavy bundles of furs were best transported in boats. The land on the west side of the Connecticut was rich and alluvial, suitable for the growing of wheat and corn. The location of Pynchon's proposed settlement, at the intersection of a number of Indian trails and near the fording places of the area rivers, was well chosen. The site was close to the Indian beaver-trapping lands and only a few miles from present-day Westfield, where the most successful Indian fur trappers, the Woronocos, lived.

Pynchon, however, was forced to relocate his trading post site to the east side of the river. In 1635 he had erected a house, prefabricated to make on-site construction easy and quick, on the south bank of the Agawam River near its junction with the Connecticut, at a place afterwards called "house meadow." Two men, left to plant spring crops and secure Pynchon's land claims, allowed some hogs, also left by Pynchon, to root in the Indian cornfields. The Indians were angry, and to pacify them Pynchon had to relocate the settlement.

On July 15, 1636, Commuck, Matanchow, and ten other Agawam Indians deeded three parcels of land to Pynchon: the Agawam meadows on the west side of the Connecticut River; the "long meadow" which included present Longmeadow, part of East Longmeadow, and Enfield, Connecticut; and a strip of land which ran from the "long meadow" to the Chicopee River. For this land Pynchon paid the Indians twenty coats, eighteen hoes and knives, and eighteen fathoms of wampum.

William Pynchon was the most important man in early Springfield. Without him the settlement, named Springfield in 1640 after Pynchon's home village in England, might have been a failure. Someone was needed to provide direction; to maintain peace with the local Indians; and to keep the small community united, growing, and prosperous. Pynchon was able to perform these tasks with great sense of purpose.

The nearest English settlement of any size was Hartford, thirty miles to the south—a day's difficult march—and a hostile competitor with Springfield in the fur trade. The plantation was an isolated community in the middle of the wilderness. It was surrounded by the Indian villages of the Pocumtuck Confederacy and could therefore be easily destroyed. Pynchon was aware of this possibility, and as the village's magistrate or judge, he strove—if the surviving court records accurately reflect his beliefs—to ensure decent treatment of the Indians by English settlers. Englishmen brought to court for abusing Indians were whipped or fined. Indian land ownership was respected scrupulously. Pynchon and others paid more than once for the same pieces of land in order to satisfy all claimants.

It was difficult for Pynchon to keep the population of the village constant or growing. Most of the men who originally settled Agawam Plantation in 1636 were gone by 1638. None of the town's founders died there. Yet Pynchon, through the importation of contract labor or indentured servants, was able to supply some of the village's manpower needs. At the termination of their contracts, laborers were usually settled on village land.

John Stewart, a blacksmith, came to Springfield as a contract laborer. Taken prisoner during one of England's wars in Scotland, he was given the choice of migrating to the New World or going to prison. Stewart was given property in the village, the blacksmith shop, and for a price, Pynchon loaned him the smithy tools when the Scot completed his seven years of indenture. The settlement thus gained new and hopefully permanent residents.

Perhaps no two events more clearly illustrate seventeenth century Puritan religious beliefs that the cases of Mary and Hugh Parsons and the publication of a book written by William Pynchon. Mary Lewis came to Springfield in 1645. She was married but had been abandoned by her husband for more than seven years. Under English law she had the right to remarry and was given permission by William Pynchon to wed Hugh Parsons, a bricklayer. The Parsons lived at the south end of town, near the mouth of the Mill River and south of it. They were neighbors to a number of families, among them the Bedorthas. In 1649 Mary appeared in court charged with criminal defamation—spreading tales of witchcraft about the widow Marshfield, Mrs. Blanche Bedortha's mother. For her gossiping Mary was fined twenty bushels of corn to be paid to the defamed widow. What began as a personality clash between two women led to one of Massachusetts's first witchcraft cases.

Both Mary and Hugh were candidates for the charge of witchcraft: Mary was mentally ill, and Hugh was quarrelsome, given to uttering vague but menacing threats to people who displeased him. In 1650 both Mary and Hugh were questioned by William Pynchon. Thirty-five people, though records are incomplete, offered testimony concerning unpleasant or unusual events which followed verbal clashes with Hugh Parsons. Parsons in effect became a scapegoat—blamed for the bad luck of others. The town's minister, Reverend George Moxon, had clashed with Parsons. Parsons had been compelled to build a chimney for Moxon according to contract. Hugh commented that the bricks would do Moxon no good, and soon after Moxon's daughters experienced fits. Sarah Edwards had sold a small amount of milk to Parsons and he wanted more. She refused, and her cow dried up after producing milk of different colors over a period of several days. Griffith Jones told of eating dinner one Sunday. He put his meal on a makeshift table, the wooden bonnet of a cradle, and then looked for two dinner knives he owned. Both were missing, so he had to eat with an old rusty knife. Jones cleaned up the dishes, cut some tobacco for his pipe, and went to feed his pig. When he returned he found all three knives together. At that moment Hugh Parsons came into the house to ask if Jones was ready to return to the meetinghouse. Jones talked to his neighbors of Parsons's bewitching the knives.

As more rumors and stories spread, Parsons was blamed for any number of happenings. Anthony Dorchester and Parsons both held an interest in a cow. When it was slaughtered both wanted the tongue, but Dorchester received it. While he was boiling it, the tongue disappeared from the pot, and Parsons was blamed. Blanche Bedortha's two-year-old child said it was afraid of Parsons's dog, but he did not own a dog. Henry Smith had refused to sell Parsons some peas in the summer of 1648. Now he remembered that two of his children had died. Hugh Parsons's chief accuser, however, was his wife, Mary. Mary also claimed that she herself could fly through the air as well as become invisible. Both Mary and Hugh Parsons were taken into custody and charged with witchcraft. Both were sent to Boston for trial. Hugh was in prison in October 1651. He was tried for witchcraft in the spring of 1652, was acquitted, and never returned to Springfield. Tradition says that he went to live in Rhode Island. In May 1651, Mary, pleading not guilty, was tried for witchcraft. She did, however, plead guilty to a charge of murder. Both of the Parsons's children had died in infancy. Mary confessed to the murder of one. She was found guilty of murder by her own confession and sentenced to hang. She died in prison of tuberculosis before the sentence was carried out.

In the late 1640s Pynchon had written a book, *The Meritorious Price of Our Redemption*. It attempted to explain the reasons for the suffering, death, and resurrection of Jesus Christ. In consultation with Puritan ministers, the General Court of Massachusetts found the book dangerous to the faith of those who read it. The General Court therefore ordered a rebuttal written, the book burned, and Pynchon summoned to Boston to correct his errors. In seventeenth-century Massachusetts the Puritan community, led by the General Court in consultation with ministers, sought to determine and to maintain the correct Puritan beliefs. This church-state cooperation was deemed necessary to avoid religious diversity which, according to the Puritans, resulted in social disruption and anarchy. In the early 1650s Pynchon returned to England. He may have gone for business reasons; or he may have feared banishment or confiscation of his properties as a result of his book. When he returned to England, Pynchon left his son John the Connecticut Valley empire—an empire based on the fur trade. During the years he had lived in the New World, William Pynchon had done well.

John Pynchon, about twenty-five years old at the time, took what his father had left him and expanded upon it. The northeast interior was rich in beaver and muskrat, so John Pynchon established trading posts throughout the area. His agents sent him thousands of furs given by the Indians in exchange for red shag woolen cloth; glass beads; and iron hatchets, which they especially prized. Springfield was a good trading post location. It was near principal Indian trails to the Dutch settlements in present-day New York and English settlements in Connecticut and around Boston. Indians from as far west as the Great Lakes came to Agawam Plantation to trade.

John Pynchon increased both his wealth and power. He controlled a large part of the Connecticut Valley's economy. He had a warehouse on the Connecticut River at a place called Warehouse Point, below the Enfield rapids, where goods brought from Europe were carted around the rapids, loaded into smaller boats, and shipped to Springfield. In turn Pynchon shipped beaver and muskrat skins in huge barrels to England. He also shipped local products such as corn, fish, and lumber to other Connecticut River towns and to Boston. As Pynchon was the only area supplier, goods which could not be homemade, such as iron pots, glass, and Indian trade items, had to be purchased from him.

By the late 1600s Springfield was John Pynchon's fief. He owned a cider mill, a turpentine plant, a blast furnace and foundry for the production of iron goods, a sawmill, and a grist mill. John employed Springfield people to make barrels, weave linen, string wampum, make glass, run his mills and store, and transport his goods by boat or cart. All of this prosperity, vitality, and employment were rooted in the fur trade. John Pynchon's death in 1702 signaled the end of an era, for the fur trade was declining as a result of overhunting and trapping. Springfield entered the eighteenth century in a state of decline because its role as a trading post was no longer necessary. The settlement no longer had an economic purpose.

The Stone Age-woodland culture of the Springfield area Indians had endured successfully for many years. The Agawams numbered about 200 people, perhaps 25 of them warriors. These people occupied the Connecticut Valley with several other small groups, all of which were interrelated through marriage: the Woronocos in Westfield; the Nonotucks in Northampton; the Pocumtucks of Deerfield; and other groups to the north of Deerfield as well as to the south of Enfield. All of these groups were Algonquian, meaning that they spoke essentially the same language. All were subject to or allied with the Pocumtucks of Deerfield, belonging to the Pocumtuck Confederacy. In mid-seventeenth-century New England these clans together numbered about 2,000 people.

Although the Pocumtucks occupied the Connecticut Valley and some of the area around it, they could not control it. Surrounded by more powerful tribes and too few in number, the Pocumtucks were in decline. They were paying tribute in corn and children to the extremely warlike and aggressive Pequots of the lower Connecticut Valley, to the Narragansetts of Rhode Island, and to the Wampanoags of eastern Massachusetts. The Pocumtucks were also subject to

The only known portrait of William Pynchon, founder of Springfield, merchant, landholder, and fur trader, hangs in the Essex Institute, Salem, Massachusetts. It was painted in 1657. The skullcap was common wear in an age of drafty fireplace-heated houses. Courtesy of Springfield City Library

the Mohawks of the Hudson Valley. The Mohawks, part of the Iroquois-speaking nation, were probably the most powerful Indian confederation in North America. Each year two old and infirm chiefs would canoe and portage down the Deerfield, Connecticut, and Agawam rivers, seeking to collect tribute. These chiefs were starkly symbolic. The Mohawks were powerful, and the Pocumtucks were too weak to resist them, even in the form of two old warriors.

In 1631, perhaps seeking to establish an alliance with the English, two valley Indians appeared in Boston. They tried to entice the English to settle in the Connecticut Valley, describing the soil as rich and fertile for planting and the streams as full of beaver. Although the Indians offered to pay tribute in furs and seed corn, the English refused to settle in the remote, unexplored wilderness of western Massachusetts. Not until the Pocumtucks had been reduced by disease would the English establish a settlement in the Springfield area. The founding or "planting" of Pynchon's Agawam Plantation may have led the Pocumtucks to believe that they now had a powerful, musket-armed ally.

Before Pynchon settled at Agawam, other Englishmen had established towns in the lower Connecticut Valley in the present state of Connecticut. These settlements were located on land occupied or controlled by the Pequots. The Pequots resented English settlement, and in 1637 war broke out. The Pocumtucks, though the Pequots sought their support, remained friendly to the English. The Pequots were defeated, their main village burned, and the survivors dispersed or sold into slavery. One enemy of the Pocumtucks was gone, probably to their relief.

William Pynchon and the other settlers at Agawam Plantation, however, never became the allies that the Agawams and other Pocumtucks may have desired. Mohawk raiding parties swept through the area, killing Pocumtucks caught alone in the forests or meadows. Rumors of approaching Mohawk war parties sent local villagers into panicked flight. Yet William Pynchon, and after him John, refused to

raise a hand in aid. The Mohawks were friendly to the English, and Pynchon had no desire for war. Since Springfield was a small, underpopulated village, a Mohawk war party could easily destroy it.

As the years passed, relations between the Indian people of the valley and the people of Springfield deteriorated. Coexistence became increasingly difficult. There were incidents of Indians stealing food, clothing, guns, and gold coins from Springfield settlers. Cases of English assaults on Agawam Indians and Indian assaults on settlement people were heard in the Springfield court. There were, however, problems apart from thievery or assault cases. The Pynchons, both William and later John, were buying more and more land from the Agawams and other valley Indians. In 1665 the Agawams discovered that they had bartered away so much land that they were unable to plant corn, their most important food. Fifteen acres of land were returned to them. Yet the loss of land continued. In 1666 John Pynchon purchased the village site of the Agawams on the west side of the Connecticut and, in exchange, built the Agawams a village at the top of "the long hill," now Longhill Street. The Agawams may have felt some resentment, since the land, once theirs, was now owned by the people of Springfield.

Apart from land loss, the Agawams, as reflected by their new English-built village, had become dependent on Springfield. On credit, the Indians bought English-made blankets, clothes, food, and tools, and, also, illegally acquired guns and liquor. If they could not pay their debts, the Agawams mortgaged future crops or lost their land. The Agawams and other Pocumtucks also farmed English-owned land for a share of the crop. They hired Englishmen to plow Indian fields. The valley Indians had willingly invited Pynchon into the valley in 1636. Now, in the late 1660s, they realized that their land, their independence, and their way of life were being lost.

By 1659 Springfield's constable was attempting to force local Indians to honor the Puritan Sunday. A group of Indians

The Hassocky Marsh looked much like this unidentified modern-day marsh. Courtesy of Springfield City Library

traveling in Westfield—an illegal act because it was a day of rest—had a gun taken away, and one of them was bitten by the constable's dog. Apart from the loss of land and the increasingly direct English influence on Indian culture, the Pocumtucks faced other English-related problems. In the early 1650s the Pocumtucks had gone to war against the Mohegan Indians of Connecticut. Since the Mohegans were allies of the English and had helped them defeat the Pequots, the English intervened and kept the Pocumtucks from victory.

In 1675 a war between the English and the Wampanoags began in eastern Massachusetts. The valley Indians paid tribute to the Wampanoags, led by Metacom, better known as King Philip, and owed allegiance to them. In August 1675 the valley tribes began to war against the English settlements of western Massachusetts. Brookfield was attacked. Northfield and Deerfield were abandoned. In September a large English force was ambushed near Deerfield and almost completely destroyed. The English were stunned. The valley Indians had always been friendly and docile. As Metacom's victories mounted, more and more valley warriors thought of war; but John Pynchon did not believe that the Agawams would join the other valley clans in war against the English. The government of Massachusetts, however, ordered him to take some Agawam hostages and send them to Hartford in order to ensure peace. The hostages were sent, though not disarmed, and were, for never-explained reasons, allowed to escape. Pynchon, however, was never advised of the hostages' release, and on October 4, 1675, he led Springfield's garrison of mounted troopers to Hadley as ordered by the authorities in Boston. Springfield was left protected by a small number of men and boys.

On Monday, October 4, 1675—October 14 according to our modern calendar, the Agawam Indians, and an unknown number of Indian allies attacked and burned Springfield. Twenty-five houses and thirty-five barns were burned in the raid. Four settlers died. Although the Indians did inflict great damage—burning the barns destroyed the community's winter food supply, the attack was a limited success. The town had been forewarned. Days before the raid an Agawam Indian woman, though her claim was discounted, warned of a coming raid, and the evening before the actual raid an Indian named Toto, living with an English family in Windsor, Connecticut—told of the impending raid. Springfield was warned by express rider that very night. The town's residents, therefore, gathered what possessions they could, moved to three fortified houses along Main Street, and awaited the attack. When morning came and the attack did not occur, the people returned to their homes. Pentacost Bond, wife of the town's drummer—he beat the drum to announce the beginning of a religious service or a town meeting because there were few, if any, clocks in the village—returned to her south end home with a small number of reconnoitering militia. Two men, Thomas Miller and Thomas Cooper, rode down Main Street and up the "long hill," intending to observe the Indian village. They were ambushed and Cooper was killed immediately. Miller, wounded, fell from his horse, remounted, was shot a second time, and, though dying, rode back to town to warn the people of the coming attack. Pentacost Bond was killed on her doorstep. Most of the residents, however, returned safely to the fortified houses.

The raid had been well planned. A militia force was at Westfield, commanded by a Major Treat. This force, however, was located on the west side of the Connecticut River. To lessen the possibility of these troops aiding Springfield, the Indians had destroyed most of the boats on the east and west sides of the river. When Treat marched to Springfield's aid, he could not cross. Three or four young men, Edmund Pangrydys among them, slipped out of one of the fortified houses, reached a canoe hidden near the river bank, and began to ferry Treat's soldiers, five or six at a time, across the Connecticut to the Springfield side. Indians along the east bank attempted, vainly, to prevent the crossings. Pangrydys

17

A picture taken in the vicinity of Bradley Road in 1934 suggests the appearance of the land east of the Hassocky Marsh in the seventeenth century. Courtesy of Springfield City Library

wounded in this action, died several days later. In response to Treat's crossing and perhaps to information that mounted troops led by John Pynchon were on their way from Hadley, the Indians ended the raid.

Little verifiable information concerning the raid exists. According to tradition Miles Morgan, whose house stood where the bus station is today, and whose statue is on Court Square, refused to abandon his house. He and his family fought off the raiding Indians and saved it. A second tradition concerns an action at John Pynchon's fortified house which once stood near the present intersection of Fort and Main streets. The Indians gained access to the main entrance and a wood framed hall running the length of the building, setting them on fire. They had to be driven out in hand-to-hand combat while the fire was extinguished.

Although the Indians burned Springfield, they did not destroy the fall harvest of hay and grain stored in West Springfield barns. That supply would keep Springfield fed. Without homes throughout a mild winter and intensely fearful of more Indian raids, the people of Springfield—most of them—remained, and over a period of years rebuilt their homes and barns.

Whatever advantages the valley Indians held at the outbreak of the war did not continue. They lacked warriors, guns, gunpowder, and food; and they suffered a major defeat at present-day Turners Falls, the site of an Indian fishing camp on the Connecticut River. John Gilbert of Springfield had been taken captive, was held at the campsite, and had escaped. He guided an army of 180 men to attack the camp. In the attack more than 300 Indian men, women, and children were killed. Yet the force of soldiers, incorrectly fearing that Metacom was approaching with 1,000 warriors, panicked and fled. The retreat turned into a rout when the camp's surviving warriors regrouped and counterattacked the fleeing soldiers. That force of soldiers would have been destroyed except for a rear-guard action organized by Samuel Holyoke

of Springfield. His actions guaranteed the survival of the English army. Several months later he died of exhaustion or wounds from the battle.

By the summer of 1675, Metacom was dead, killed by a fellow Indian. The Pocumtucks—the Agawams among them—fled the valley in small groups, retreating through the Berkshire hills into New York and eventually into Canada. Many were killed on the way by colonial militia or died of starvation and disease. Captured survivors were sold into slavery in the Caribbean. After the war only a few Agawams returned to the Springfield area, several living on the Pecousic Brook in Forest Park until the time of the American Revolution. Over a period of forty years, valley Indian culture was gradually subverted and overwhelmed. By 1675 many Springfield-area Indians hunted with English guns, wore English clothes, and worshipped the English god. The war of 1675-76, more commonly called King Philip's War, ultimately secured the continued existence and expansion of English culture in New England. That war ended, forever, the ancient ways of the Agawams, the Nonotucks, and other valley Indian clans.

The Birth of Springfield, *painted in 1909 by Jonas J. LaValle, barber and self-taught artist, shows seventeenth-century Agawam Plantation. Although the painting is inaccurate, it does portray the openness and limited development of early Springfield. The narrow, fence-lined path in front of the houses is present-day Main Street. The painting, recently restored, hangs in the mayor's office. Courtesy of Springfield City Library*

The Brewer kitchen, a period room in the Connecticut Valley Historical Museum at the Quadrangle, shows the close, dark, closet-free atmosphere of a late-seventeenth–early-eighteenth-century Springfield house. The room, brought from Connecticut and installed when the museum was built in 1927, is furnished with seventeenth-century items. Courtesy of Connecticut Valley Historical Museum

Built in 1645 at the southeast corner of present-day Court Square by Thomas Cooper with the help of townspeople, the first meetinghouse was Springfield's religious and social center. The picture is probably inaccurate. The towers were directly on the roof, one forward of the other; one was a lookout, the other a bell tower. Drawing by Catherine Y. Reinhardt, 1936; courtesy of Springfield City Library

The houses of early settlers were wood frame and batten board with woven straw roofs. Pen and ink sketch by Carol P. Petell, 1984

*B*uilt in 1677, the second parsonage was forty-nine feet long and twenty feet wide. Drawing by Wallace E. Dibble, 1936; courtesy of Springfield City Library

*O*ne of the first buildings constructed by William Pynchon was a trading house. The building was located at the foot of present-day Longhill Street. Indians from New York, Connecticut, and Massachusetts journeyed here to exchange furs for trade items. William Pynchon is directly to the left of Captain John Mason who wears a sword. Illustration by F. T. Merril, from Charles H. Barrow's The History of Springfield for the Young, 1923; from the author's collection

*D*emolished in 1884, this garrison house once stood near the present corner of Main and Loring streets. In the mid-seventeenth century it was owned by Margaret, the widow of Thomas Bliss of Hartford. In 1645 Margaret Bliss and eight of her children walked five days from Hartford through the wilderness to settle in Springfield. Both Margaret and Bliss streets, laid out in the nineteenth century across Margaret Bliss's land, were named after her. Sketch by Wallace E. Dibble, 1936; courtesy of Springfield City Library

*T*hese two buildings, the old Blake house and the Ely Ordinary, were drawn in pen and ink in 1893 prior to their demolition. The Blake house dated to the mid-eighteenth century. The Ely Tavern or ordinary, which dated back to the late seventeenth century, once stood on the corner of Elm and Main streets, and was owned by Samuel Ely. In the seventeenth century ordinaries were important to community life. Ely's was subsidized by the town to keep it open, and he was released from training day or militia duty to operate it. Drawing by George C. Gardiner, 1893; courtesy of Springfield City Library

In the mid-1630s the Dutch of New York claimed the Connecticut Valley as their territory. The Dutch map shows William Pynchon's Agawam Plantation, "Mr. Pincer's handel house," and his settlement at Warehouse Point, Connecticut, "Mr. Pincer's cleine val." Courtesy of Springfield City Library

Some of Springfield's early settlers walked to the plantation from the Boston area, a trek of 100 miles taking ten days to two weeks. Few of these people were wilderness-wise, relying on Indian guides. Such weapons as the blunderbuss, held by the man in the center of the picture, were uncommon. The usual weapon was a flintlock musket. Wash drawing by Charles G. Copeland from Mason Green's Springfield, 1636-1886, History of Town and City; from the author's collection

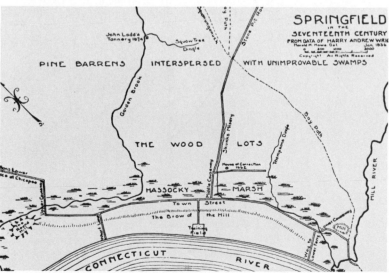

Harry Andrew Wright, an avid local historian of a generation ago, carefully researched and drew this map of early seventeenth-century Springfield. The map shows the island upon which William Pynchon located Agawam Plantation. The roads west and east of the "town street" are late seventeenth- or early eighteenth-century. Until causeways—earthen bridges—were constructed, the early settlement was most conveniently reached by boat. Courtesy of Springfield City Library

People who were odd-looking or eccentric could be accused of "familiarity with the devil" as in the cases of Mary and Hugh Parsons. Sketch by Robert Holcomb; from the author's collection

THE
MERITORIOUS PRICE
OF
Our Redemption, Iuftification, &c.

Cleering it from fome common Errors;

And proving,

Part I. {
1. That Chrift did not fuffer for us thofe unutterable torments of Gods wrath, that commonly are called Hell-torments, to redeem our foules from them.
2. That Chrift did not bear our fins by Gods imputation, and therefore he did not bear the curfe of the Law for them.

Part II. {
3. That Chrift hath redeemed us from the curfe of the Law (not by fuffering the faid curfe for us, but) by a fatisfactory price of attonement; *viz.* by paying or performing unto his Father that invaluable precious thing of his Mediatoriall obedience, wherof his Mediatoriall Sacrifice of attonement was the mafter-piece.
4. A finners righteoufneffe or juftification is explained, and cleered from fome common Errors.

By *William Pincbin*, Gentleman, in New-England.

The Mediator faith thus to his Father in *Pfal* 40.8,10.
I delight to do thy will O my God, yea thy Law is within my heart : (*viz.*) I delight to do thy will, or Law, as a Mediator.
I have not hid thy righteoufneffe within my heart, I have declared thy faithfulneffe, and thy falvation: Namely, I have not hid thy righteoufneffe, or thy way of making finners righteous, but have declared it by the performance of my Mediatoriall Sacrifice of attonement, as the procuring caufe of thy attonement, to the great Congregation for their everlafting righteoufneffe.

LONDON.
Printed by *F. M.* for *George Whittington*, and *James Moxon*, and are to be fold at the blue Anchor in Corn-hill neer the Royall Exchange. 1650.

The title page of William Pynchon's book, The Meritorious Price of Our Redemption, *published in 1650, shows why the book was burned by the public executioner on Boston Common. In denying that Christ suffered "hell-torments" for human sin, Pynchon was denying basic Puritan religious doctrine. Courtesy of Springfield City Library*

The Puritan, a bronze sculpture by August Saint-Gaudens, represents the spirit and determination of Springfield's early settlers. The statue is of Deacon Samuel Chapin (1598-1675), who came to Springfield in 1643. He was appointed to Springfield's first board of selectmen and was given the title "Deacon" when he began to conduct Sunday services. The sculpture stands west of the Springfield City Library on State Street. Courtesy of Stanislaus J. Skarzynski

John Pynchon is here presented in a highly idealistic fashion as a dedicated young scholar pursuing his lessons. Illustration by F. L. Merrill from Charles H. Barrow's The History of Springfield for the Young, *1923; from the author's collection*

Boston's public executioner burns Pynchon's book on Boston Common. Illustration by F. L. Merrill from Barrow's The History of Springfield for the Young, *1923; from the author's collection*

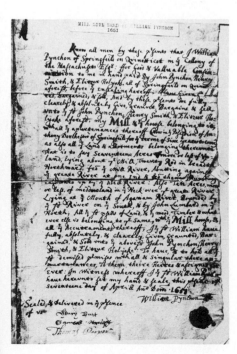

Before William Pynchon returned to England he deeded his New World holdings to his son John and his sons-in-law Henry Smith and Elizur Holyoke. With this deed he transferred the ownership of a Mill River mill "with apurtenaces"—equipment, a house, and about twenty-seven acres of land on both sides of the "great river," the Connecticut. Courtesy of Springfield City Library

John Pynchon recorded his business dealings in a number of account books dating from 1650 to 1680. All dealings—contracts, memorandums, receipts—were put in writing. Since paper was scarce, all space was used. The covers, the flyleaves, and the insides of the covers were written on, making a jumble of notations. The account books are in the collection of the Connecticut Valley Historical Museum at the Quadrangle. Courtesy of Springfield City Library

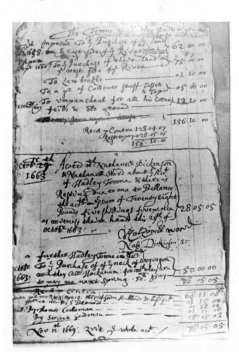

This Milton Bradley Company print shows the company's nineteenth-century factory in an insert and John Pynchon's seventeenth-century "mansion house" or "old fort." The house was built about 1660, of bricks made in Northampton (50,000 of them) and stood about seventy feet back from Main Street with its south wall on Fort Street. The first-floor walls were two feet thick. The building was called the "old fort," hence Fort Street, because it was a place of refuge for the town's settlers during King Philip's War in 1675. Courtesy of Springfield City Library

Miles Morgan was an early settler, arriving in Springfield in the late 1630s. During the Indian raid of 1675, he was in command of the Old Fort. His house stood near the present-day corner of Main and Liberty streets, the present location of the bus station. Morgan's statue, by J. S. Hartley, is on Court Square in front of the old city hall. Courtesy of Springfield City Library

Little remains of seventeenth-century Springfield except for a few tombstones in area cemeteries. Mary Holyoke was the daughter of William Pynchon and became the wife of Elizur Holyoke. Courtesy of Springfield City Library

The Indian stockade, once located at the top of Longhill Street, was English-planned and built in exchange for the Agawam Indians' planting grounds and village site west of the Connecticut River and south of the Agawam River. The oval stockade, built in 1666 by John Pynchon, stood on a hill 136 feet above the Connecticut. A narrow path with a ravine on either side led to the village. The excavations of 1895 uncovered twenty-six fire holes, indicating a village of perhaps 200 people. From Charles H. Barrow's The History of Springfield for the Young, 1923, artist unknown; from the author's collection

In the spring of 1895 Dr. Philip Kilroy announced that he would build a house, now the property of the Vincentian Fathers, on what was known as the Storrs Lot on Longhill Street. The site had been the location of a seventeenth-century Indian village. Permission was granted to do an archaeological dig, and Lewis C. Grant, who participated in the dig, drew this diagram. The numbers on the diagram represent the location of bones of sheep, hog, and deer which were found in fire pits; seventeenth-century Dutch clay pipes and other artifacts, both Indian and European, were also found. Courtesy of Springfield City Library

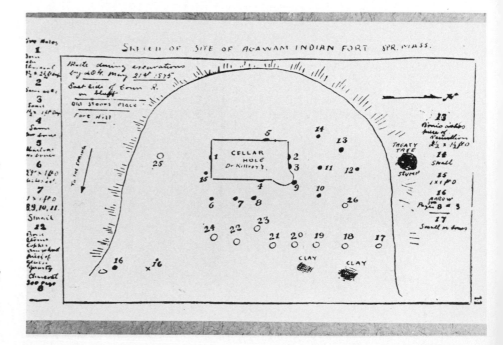

Before European contact the Agawam Indians wore primarily animal skins in winter and went nearly naked in summer. Pen and ink sketch by Carol P. Petell, 1984

The wigwam was easily constructed of saplings set upright in the ground, lashed together at their tops, and then covered with grass mats or animal hides, and could be quickly constructed or dismantled. In summer the sides could be rolled up to allow a breeze to enter. In winter, with mats or hides secured, the wigwam was warm though full of smoke from an always-burning fire and poor ventilation. Pen and ink sketch by Milton Bradley, founder of the Milton Bradley Company, date unknown; courtesy of Springfield City Library

In 1636-37 the Pequot War was fought in the southern Connecticut Valley, a preview of events which would occur later in the century in the Springfield area. The Pequots were almost completely destroyed. After the war Connecticut's settlers faced starvation. Corn was bought from the Indians in the greater Springfield area at high and sometimes prepaid prices. These arrangements caused friction between Springfield and Hartford.

Hartford believed that William Pynchon was attempting to profit from Connecticut's need, because he tried to discourage the trading. Pynchon believed that Hartford was inflating the price of corn and making it more difficult for Agawam Plantation to deal with the valley Indians. The result of the so-called Corn Controversy was an intense rivalry between Hartford and Springfield, especially in the fur trade. Ultimately Springfield, which once had close ties to Connecticut, gave its allegiance to Boston and remained part of Massachusetts rather than becoming a part of Connecticut. *From Charles H. Barrow's* The History of Springfield for the Young, *1923, artist unknown; from the author's collection*

Shortly after English settlement of the valley, the Indians adopted European-style clothing, which was superior to animal skins. Pen and ink sketch by Carol P. Petell

Massasoit chief as first
seen by the Englishman
Edward Winslow March 22.
1621.

*This picture of Massasoit, the great
sachem of the Wampanoag Indians of
eastern Rhode Island and Massachusetts,
was used on special event menus at the
Massasoit House. The picture was
supposedly done from life in 1621.
Courtesy of Springfield City Library*

Metacom or Metacomet (called Philip), son of the great sachem Massasoit, led his people in an unsuccessful war to drive the English out of Massachusetts in what today is known as King Philip's War. Engraving by Paul Revere; courtesy of Springfield City Library

John Pynchon led mounted troops on a ride from Hadley to Springfield when he learned of the Indian raid. He was much too late to help. Illustration by Charles Copeland from Mason Green's Springfield, 1636-1886, History of Town and City, 1886; from the author's collection

Lieutenant Cooper and Constable Miller were ambushed while attempting to reconnoiter the Indian village the morning of the Indian raid on Springfield. From Charles H. Barrow's History of Springfield for the Young, 1923, artist unknown; from the author's collection

The Eighteenth Century:
Life In A Colonial Town

Chapter Two

The town of Springfield entered the eighteenth century with the negative heritage of the collapse of the fur trade and the infertility of the soil. But there were other problems retarding the town's development. Springfield was located on a river 500 yards wide in some places. Yet the rapids at Enfield, Connecticut, made a direct link between the Atlantic Ocean and Springfield difficult; the river above Hartford was less than ten feet deep in places and unnavigable to anything other than a flatboat or sloop. Perhaps the most important reason for Springfield's poor growth was its location on the Massachusetts frontier. From 1675 until 1760 New England was plagued with war. Agawam Indian warriors burned Springfield in 1675; and as late as 1742 French and Indian raiding parties from Canada came to the area intent on destroying valley settlements. For more than half of the eighteenth century, Springfield was a fortified town. Houses were built with heavy wooden doors and shutters. The meetinghouse on present-day Court Street had a palisade wall three-quarters of the way around it. People feared attack, and for years vigilant men patrolled to the north and west, seeking evidence that French and Indian war parties were in the vicinity.

Paradoxically, Springfield's continued existence, poor development, and lack of population was due to this continued warfare—actual or threatened. Springfield became an important frontier outpost. Both militia and military supplies were gathered here for campaigns against the French and Indians. Finally, in 1763, the British conquered French Canada. The last of a series of North American wars between France and England was over. Springfield now became an unimportant village on the Connecticut River, no longer necessary to any war effort.

As the seventeenth century ended and the eighteenth began, the town's appearance had not changed. Springfield's center was still split by a single street with house lots to the west and the marsh to the east. As in the previous century, each lot contained a house, barns, perhaps an orchard, a vegetable garden, and a cornfield. Farm families continued to spin and weave flax, tan leather, and make rude furniture for their own use. In essence Springfield was a tightly-knit village, a narrow society peopled by the descendants of seventeenth-century Puritans, laboring for their daily bread and reading the Bible to discover God's will. Government policies reinforced the close-knit nature of the town. The Massachusetts General Court allowed the towns of the colony to dispose of land, levy local taxes, choose town officers, and conduct town meetings. People, according to both tradition and government policy, were therefore only interested in local affairs, leaving the complexities of provincial and imperial matters to Springfield's representatives in the general court.

Yet within this traditional environment change was occurring. Orthodox Puritanism, basic to the life style just described, was in transition. Throughout Massachusetts the stern Puritanism of the 1600s was easing. Non-church members could hold public office. Public declaration of sins was no longer necessary to become a communicant; babies that were products of seven-month marriages were allowed baptism; and the children of fathers who were not members of a congregation could be baptized—if their grandfathers had been church members.

Robert Breck, appointed minister to Springfield in 1734, typified all of these changes. Breck, a native of Marlborough and a Harvard graduate, believed that Christ was not divine, that non-Christians could be saved, and that adulteresses could be forgiven; and, though records are not complete, he appears to have been welcome in the town. More conservative ministers from Connecticut and Boston had him arrested for preaching "dangerous" ideas. In fact, his house was surrounded by an armed posse and he was escorted to jail. Ultimately the civil authorities refused to prosecute, and Breck returned in 1736 to Springfield to become minister. During this period, Stephen Williams, Longmeadow minister and not a friend of Breck's, wrote in his diary that people were unbaptized, dressed extravagantly, were publicly drunk, rarely attended Sunday meeting, and committed adultery and fornication. The power of Puritan orthodoxy was declining.

By the mid-eighteenth century, Springfield's population was clustered along seven narrow and unpaved streets in the center of what today is called "downtown." The center had not changed much since the time of John Pynchon 100 years earlier. Main Street still ran on the western edge of the Hassocky Marsh, which covered the earth between the present Carew Street to the north, Winchester Square to the east, and State Street to the south. Springfield's largest concentration of buildings was along the "town street," Main Street. A row of homes and businesses was located on the west side of the street. Few buildings stood on the east side because of the marsh and the town brook, which ran next to the road. Buildings on the east side were reached by narrow planks crossing the brook, and some of these buildings were elevated on pilings to avoid flooding when water in the marsh was high.

Springfield center had two residential-business concentrations. The first was located near the present corner of State and Main streets, the second near the present Cypress Street. A number of homes and businesses clustered around the town's courthouse near State and Main streets. This building stood near the present site of the Northeast Federal Savings Bank. It was on the other side of the town brook and could be reached by a plank bridge. In front of the courthouse stood a whipping post, and to the east of it stood the town's one-room schoolhouse. All of these buildings were wooden except for John Pynchon's brick house, the Old Fort, near the present corner of Main and Fort streets. Most were weathered gray or brown, but a few were painted white, yellow, or red.

Directly on the corner of State and Main streets stood the general store of Jonathan Dwight. The building was wooden, painted red, and two stories high. There Dwight sold gunpowder, bolts of cloth, medicine, and millstones. He was perhaps the most prosperous storekeeper in the community.

Dwight lived near his store on the north side of Maple Street near the present corner of High Street. At that time, Willow Street and the other streets behind McDonald's did not exist. On that land Dwight maintained flower and vegetable gardens down to the present South Main Street. Through these gardens flowed a brook which Dwight used as a water supply. He also owned the land which the present Chestnut Street crosses. In fact, Dwight laid out Chestnut Street. This land was heavily treed. Where the city library is today stood giant oaks, willows, and elms. Clear springs bubbled from the ground among the trees, feeding water to the marsh and keeping it fresh and free of stagnation.

Dwight was a hard worker, noted for tending his livestock on cold winter mornings while only half dressed. After such a morning, he would have to rub the circulation back into his legs. Once he reminisced to a friend that in 1753 Springfield had only one clock, which Josiah Dwight, his uncle, owned. People would call at his uncle's house to hear it chime the hours. Some would gather around the front door if they could not get in, and others would just happen to pass by on the hour for a visit.

Jonathan Dwight held Tory views at the beginning of the American Revolution. Believing that all his property was to be seized by the Revolutionary government, he ordered his slave, Andrew, to drive all his cattle over the Connecticut line. Dwight was to follow with whatever valuables he could carry. Fortunately his wife persuaded him not to leave. Eventually he accepted the Revolution and American independence, and he continued to be Springfield's leading merchant.

Luke Bliss lived on the southeast corner of Main and State streets across from Dwight's store. He sang in the church choir. He and his brother, Jonathan Bliss, owned hundreds of acres of land lying on the high ground between the present Springfield Technical Community College grounds and the Watershops and eastward. But the land was not fertile. It was sandy, full of scrub pine and bushes, and not worth more than a few pennies an acre in the 1770s.

Continuing north up the "town street," beyond the Dwight store and the courthouse, was Parsons Tavern. The tavern was located on the southeast corner of the present Court Square. It was a popular gathering place for travelers and townspeople. Behind the tavern and facing the present Elm Street was the town church, a simple, white, steepled

building. Within it were rows of uncomfortable wooden pews. There were no religious symbols, just a pulpit. The building was not heated in winter, not because the minister wanted his congregation cold, but because fireplaces were dangerous. No building could have a fireplace unless there was always someone there to see that the fire did not get out of control and burn the structure. To compensate for the cold, the minister wore woolen mittens and the congregation used foot warmers.

Going north on the town street, beyond the church and on the west side, was the shop of Moses Church, a hatter. Church was Springfield's first postmaster. Hats and rum were sold on one side of his shop, and mail was taken in on the other. In those days whoever received mail paid postage.

The Worthington Tavern, on the west side of Main Street, was on the lot between the present Bridge and Worthington streets. At that time Bridge Street did not exist, and Worthington Street was only a narrow path leading from the tavern to the barns and other buildings on the mostly vacant land behind the tavern. The building was owned by John Worthington, Springfield's most influential and wealthiest man at that time. He was college-educated, a lawyer, and an aristocrat. He was not long in the tavern business because, some said, he disliked mixing drinks for the customers, feeling it was beneath his dignity. Eventually he converted the tavern into a private home and lived in it.

During the early 1770s there were no buildings on the east side of Main Street from opposite Pynchon Street, behind city hall, to Carew Street in the North End because of the marsh. A second cluster of buildings was located further north around Ferry Lane, now Liberty Street. Ferry Lane was Springfield's second business-residential center because the ferry crossed the river to West Springfield at that point. The wagon trade between Springfield and Hartford, or Hartford and Hadley, crossed the river there. To serve this wagon trade, small shops, taverns, and the homes of the people who owned these businesses were built near Ferry Lane.

Dr. Charles Pynchon lived on the south corner of Ferry Lane where it merged with Main Street. He also had an office and a drugstore at this location. Zebina Stebbins, a storekeeper, lived on the north corner of Ferry Lane and was apparently unhappy because Pynchon's building blocked his view of the Connecticut River. So Stebbins leased, for 999 years, a parcel of land on the east side of Main Street to Pynchon and moved Pynchon's house to this new location.

Further north, near the present corner of Main and Sargent streets, was Joseph Stebbins's tavern, where some drank too much and too loudly while sitting before Stebbins's fireplace. When this occurred, Stebbins, who was a major in the local militia, would get angry, pick up a chair, and rush them with it, scattering most and bruising some. A man of few words, he was announcing, in effect, that the hour was

Province of the **Massachusetts-Bay,**

WILLIAM SHIRLEY, Esq; Captain-General and Governour in Chief, in and over His Majesty's Province of the *Massachusetts-Bay* in *New-England, &c.*

To *Phinehas Chapin Gentleman* ——— Greeting.

BY Virtue of the Power and Authority, in and by His Majesty's Royal Commission to Me granted to be Captain General, &c. over this His Majesty's Province of the *Massachusetts-Bay*, aforesaid ; I (by these Presents) reposing especial Trust and Confidence in your Loyalty, Courage and good Conduct, constitute and appoint You the said *Phinehas Chapin* to be *Ensign of the Foot Company in the Town of Springfield* under the command of *Captain Senezer Hitchcock* in the *South Regiment* of Militia within the County of *Hampshire* whereof *is the* Esq; Colonel.

You are therefore carefully and diligently to discharge the Duty of an *Ensign* in leading, ordering and exercising said *Company* in Arms, both Inferiour Officers and Soldiers, and to keep them in good Order and Discipline ; hereby commanding them to obey you as their *Ensign* and your self to observe and follow such Orders and Instructions, as you shall from time to time receive from Me, or the Commander in Chief for the Time being, or other your superiour Officers for His Majesty's Service, according to military Rules and Discipline pursuant to the Trust reposed in You.

Given under My Hand & Seal at Arms at Boston, the Twenty Eighth Day of August in the Twenty Eighth Year of the Reign of His Majesty King George the Second, Annoq; Domini, 1754.

By His Excellency's Command, *J. Willard Secy.*

W Shirley

---

late and the tavern was closing. During the Revolution the cellar of the tavern became a storehouse for rum and molasses captured from the British. These supplies were moved to Springfield to keep the British from recapturing them, and they were used by Springfield's garrison of troops.

Opposite the Stebbins tavern was the house of Joseph Carew, a tanner. Anyone wanting leather tanned would be sent to him by Stebbins. Carew in turn would announce that the leather would not be ready until the following day and direct his customer to stay overnight at Stebbins's tavern, calling it the best lodging in town. Stebbins and Carew would later divide the profits. However, that was not all. Carew would make sure the tanned leather was dampened in a brook before he weighed it and set his fee.

Just south of Stebbins's tavern was the home of Captain Thomas Stebbins. He had a pottery on the east side of the "town street" and used clay brought by wagon from "the long hill" where Longhill Street is today. The clay was pulverized in a circular trough in the ground by rolling a millstone around a point in the center. The millstone lay near Main Street until about 1868 when it was used for a doorstep foundation.

A principal reason why this second business district of Revolution-era Springfield prospered was the presence of the original Springfield Armory. A number of buildings in the vicinity of the present Emory Street were leased by the Revolutionary government of Massachusetts. Here musket cartridges were made. Nearby were barracks for soldiers and barns for their horses. As the war continued, more buildings were leased by the government for the repair and storage of military supplies. Ferry Lane and Springfield consequently prospered.

There were few roads beyond Springfield center. Springfield was underpopulated and underdeveloped, so there was no reason for roads. Besides, there were few buildings except on farms beyond the village's center. There was little on the hill where Winchester Square is located today. As if to emphasize its isolation and lack of development, State Street was simply known as "the road" as late as 1813.

Actually, State Street's location in the 1770s was different than it is today. To avoid the steepness of State Street hill, now graded, the road ran from State Street south on Myrtle Street then east on High Street, behind the present day Wesson Hospital, to Walnut Street then back to State Street. At that time High Street was a ravine with a brook running through it, so it was not a very steep roadway. The land on either side of upper State Street was unappealing because it was wet, containing springs and ponds. Spring Street, behind Technical High School, was named for the large number of springs that flowed out of the slope above the marsh. Springfield center was surrounded by damp, boggy land from Chicopee to Longmeadow.

The roads of Revolutionary-period Springfield are difficult to identify because Springfield streets had no formal names until 1826. Before that date existing streets might have had several names. For example, Carew Street in the 1770s was known as the Upper Causeway, the Skipmunck Road, Chicopee Road, and Northeast Street. It was called the Upper Causeway because a log roadway and a bridge crossed the marsh just above where Carew Street meets Main Street today. It was known as Skipmunck Road because it also led to Chicopee Falls, then called Skipmunck; and it was also known as Northeast Street because that was its general direction. Carew Street was part of the road which led from Hadley to the Connecticut line at Warehouse Point in East Windsor. Wagons using the road carried corn, rye, wheat, dried peas, salt pork, hams, bacon, some beaver skins, tanned leather, and hides to Warehouse Point. They returned with sugar, molasses, rum, spices, nails, and bolts of cloth.

Carew Street's original residences were located on the north side of the street. A part of the large swamp which also bordered Main Street was called the Muxey Swamp. It was on the south side of Carew Street, one of the few roads which led

A view of Mount Tom and the Connecticut River, done about 1837-1838, shows the most common type of river transportation in the eighteenth and early nineteenth centuries. Painting by Thomas Creswick from a sketch by William H. Bartlett; courtesy of Springfield City Library

out of town, and Liberty Street was then a part of it.

After every rain Carew became a morass of soft, sticky, deep mud. Teamster wagons using the road would bog down, and people living in the vicinity profited by hauling these wagons free of the mud. Lower State Street's condition on rainy days only increased Carew Street's traffic confusion. Lower State Street would flood, and teamsters would detour up Carew to get across the marsh, creating a great traffic snarl.

Even when the original street names have survived, the streets' original routes have long since disappeared. A trip up present Maple Street will help illustrate the point. Maple Street was once the "road to Charley Brewer's" and stopped at the corner of Avon Place. During the 1700s it probably ran westward of its present location. In those days Maple Street hill was very steep. To avoid the steepness, the townspeople developed a winding, narrow, indirect path around the crown of Maple Hill. In its time, Maple Street has been straightened, graded, widened, and hardened, as well as lengthened. As late as 1964 lower Maple Street was widened, and in 1971 a ramp leading from Dwight Street was added. It is easy to speak of Maple Street as "the road to Charley Brewer's," but it is more difficult, and probably impossible, to know fully the course of this early road. Maple Street is named after the maple trees which lined the lane in colonial days. Planted by Charley Brewer in the 1770s, most have been cut down over the years. Today a better name would probably be Medical Center Avenue.

Isolated farms were scattered throughout Springfield in the 1770s. Some of these were connected by narrow, winding paths which eventually became public roads. In the middle 1880s Allen Street was described as dotted with scrub pine and some stands of oak and chestnut. Dickinson Street at the same time was described as an "ancient" unnamed road. The roads got their names because one ran through the farmland of Joel (or Joseph) Allen and the other through the land of Dickinson. Neither seems to have been much more than a path.

Belmont Avenue existed in the 1770s but was known as Blake Road because the Blake family owned a farmhouse at the corner of Belmont Avenue and Fort Pleasant Avenue. Little is known about the Blakes, whose house was supposed to be haunted by the ghost of someone murdered there. On the right, going up Belmont Hill, is Blake Place; so the old name still survives.

Below Belmont Hill is Locust Hill on South Main Street. Once a ledge of sandstone crowned a steep hill, which made it impossible for city businessmen of the nineteenth century to develop that portion of the South End. In 1955 Sterling Orr leveled the top of the hill by blasting, and now Cadillacs are sold there.

Plumtree Road in Sixteen Acres may have existed as early as the 1660s and is mentioned in the town records of 1706-07. Plum trees do grow in the Springfield area and did during the colonial period. In the 1880s Plumtree Road was described as sandy and winding, both hot and dusty in the summer and cold and muddy in the winter. Partridge and small game roamed the woods on either side of the road. During the same period there was a dense forest full of great wild vines, probably grape, on Plumtree near the Allen Street junction. Nearby was an area called the dunes because the sand was so concentrated that it piled in that manner.

In the early 1930s Plumtree Road was graded and somewhat straightened. Before that time Plumtree Road curved, twisted, and passed through several gullies. In 1962 Plumtree from Allen to Bradley Road was widened and resurfaced to eliminate a dangerous curve.

Sumner Avenue was a winding, narrow, dirt road called the X Road because it crossed Dickinson Street. In 1897 the X was overgrown with scrub pine and raspberry bushes. It is possible that the area was like that 125 years earlier. One of the farms on X Road was the Lombard place. The house itself was built by Daniel Lombard about 1700 and burned in 1880. It stood on the east side of the present Cherryvale

The house of Reuben Bliss, a cabinetmaker, formerly stood on the corner of Main and Montpelier streets. A paneled parlor, presently in the Smithsonian Institution, was once thought to be from this house, which was demolished about 1925. Drawing by Wallace E. Dibble, 1936; courtesy of Springfield City Library

Avenue. This road was off another lane which led from south Main Street to Pecousic Brook below Barney Hill in Forest Park. Little is known about the house except that it was two stories high and that the second floor contained a weaving room with looms and spinning wheels.

To the south of the house were a carpenter shop, blacksmith shop, and cider mill. The road which ran to the south of the house continued through apple orchards, pasture land, and wood lots, and today would be within the limits of Forest Park. The farm itself may have been sixty acres in size. To the north the house was screened by a row of Lombardy poplars and to the east, near X Road, it was screened by hawthorn trees.

During one of the Indian wars, Lombard, the owner of the farm, was working in his fields. He discovered an Indian, armed with a bow and arrow, stalking him. He had his musket with him and in turn began to stalk the Indian. This stalking and counter-stalking went on for a period of time. Both men, fearful of shooting first and missing, continued to stalk each other. Finally the Indian disappeared into the woods. The image of Indian and farmer cautiously trying to kill each other in the midst of a cornfield does illustrate the danger of frontier living in Springfield during the seventeenth and the first half of the eighteenth centuries.

Springfield's population in 1765 was approximately 2,755. By 1776, with West Springfield and Ludlow new and independent townships, it had fallen to about 2,000 living in not more than 200 houses spread over an area larger than present-day Springfield. The town was arranged like other New England villages of the period. There was a center where the church, the minister's home, and the cemetery were located. Nearby was a school, a courthouse, a number of dry goods stores, some taverns, and an apothecary shop. Randomly scattered among these buildings were private homes. All of the principal town roads converged directly or indirectly on this center and still do. Maple Street, State Street, Carew Street, and Main Street existed in those days,

though they were much narrower and had different, more informal names.

Springfield center had far more open space than it does today. It included the present Court Square and the building lots now abutting the square. It also included the corner of State and Main streets and, to the east of Main Street, the large and deep marsh. Off by itself to the north was a kind of sub-center near the present Liberty Street.

Beyond the center were many farms, some 100 acres in size, and bordering some of these farms was the outward common. This was town land being held for future town use. The people could gather firewood and graze their livestock there. In the 1770s the outward common was broken up and sold to town residents.

Before the Revolution, there was little crime in Springfield. People were not concerned about security, and doors were left open. Burglary was rare and murder very unusual. On December 13, 1770, William Shaw of Palmer, a shoemaker and father of eleven children, was hanged at the gallows tree which once stood across the street from the present High School of Commerce. Shaw, "a man of excitable temper," had been arrested for debt. While at work with shoemaking tools he had an argument with his cellmate, Edward East, and killed him with a hammer. Many people attended the hanging out of a sense of curiosity or a need for entertainment. A sermon was delivered warning people about leading a life of crime. Tradition says that Shaw tried to escape on the day of his execution by dressing in the clothes of his wife, who visited him. Wearing his wife's riding hood, he got by the jailer, but he looked back, was recognized, and was returned to his cell. Friends buried him in Palmer. Most crimes, however, were not as serious as murder, and most offenders were fined or publicly whipped. The whipping post stood in front of the courthouse as a reminder to the people to keep the law. Confining lawbreakers to jail was not a community practice in eighteenth-century Springfield.

The town of Springfield had a tradition of self-

Built about 1722, the Josiah Dwight house once stood on Main Street, at that time called "the highway," near the present corner of Howard Street. Dwight was a successful merchant, owning a general store, a gin distillery, and a "third part" of an ironworks at the "lower end of the Parish and in the Mill River." The house was moved to Historic Deerfield Village, Deerfield, Massachusetts, and is presently known as the Dwight-Barnard house. Photo courtesy of John Polak

government. The government of Massachusetts had allowed colonial towns to run their own affairs for more than 100 years. If a man owned enough property, he could vote in town meetings and hold town offices. Meetings were held at various times during the year to discuss and solve any town problems, and each year a special town meeting was held to elect town officers called selectmen, who ran town affairs for one year. The town meeting also voted to fill from their members other town offices, such as constable and road surveyor.

A major consequence of town meeting government was parochialism. Traditionally, people were only interested in local affairs. One of the biggest issues confronting the Springfield town meeting before the American Revolution was not British taxation, but a purely local issue. The question hotly debated was whether the present West Springfield should be allowed to split away from the parent town. Events irrelevant to town life were ignored. If Boston was rioting over the Stamp Act in 1765, it was no affair of Springfield's.

Parochialism was increased by a sense of isolation. Boston lay 100 miles to the east. Commercially, Springfield's lines of communication ran north-south along the Connecticut River, not east-west. A regular stage connection between Springfield and Boston was not made until the early 1780s, although a post between New York and Boston had been running for 100 years. By stage Springfield was still eighteen hours away from Boston. Even a trip to Hartford meant staying overnight in that town.

Before the 1790s only three roads led beyond Springfield: the Boston Road, connecting Boston to Hartford and running through Springfield; the Albany-New York Road; and the road to Hadley. Most town roads in those days were really short, narrow, local paths people took from the town center, for example, to reach their farms.

Most Springfield people practiced one religion, Congregationalism, and almost everyone was English in origin.

The town was a closed society to anyone who was "different." An Italian Catholic living in Springfield in 1776 would have been a curiosity. Since the town was so unified, those who were not wanted were "warned out"—told to leave—a practice which continued into the early 1800s. Many Springfield people were not happy about the Federal Armory locating in Springfield in 1794 because they feared outsiders. Strangers would flood the town looking for jobs, and Springfield's small population would then suffer political and religious divisions in its traditional way of life.

Wealthy men tended to control town politics. They not only dominated town meetings, but they were reelected time and again to the Massachusetts House of Representatives or the Governor's Council. They were the merchants, the lawyers, the prosperous farmers of the town. John Worthington, Jonathan Bliss, and Moses Bliss dominated Springfield politics. They enjoyed it. They could afford the time and, if in the Massachusetts legislature, the money to travel to Boston.

People who were not wealthy were called middling folk. These made up the bulk of Springfield's population. They were small farmers, day laborers, or modestly successful storekeepers. These people were concerned with earning their living by hard hand labor. They had little free time, and read little beyond the Bible. They had little concern for the outside world. Many were indifferent to politics, and did not attend or vote in town meetings. They wanted to dress as well as the wealthier town residents, but they did not have the money. They copied clothing styles, but the cloth was usually wool or linen.

Townspeople wore nightcaps to bed and used heavy blankets called bed rugs. Warming pans were also commonly used. A warming pan was a brass or copper pot with a hinged cover on the end of a pole. It was filled with hot ashes and pushed up and down between the sheets to warm up the bed.

There were two other classes of people living in Springfield, but little is known of either the poor white or the

black population. Apparently poor whites did some farming and day laboring. They owned little land, renting it from more prosperous neighbors. They lived in small, one-room, dirt-floored houses, little better than shacks. Blacks existed in the community as both slaves and free men. Most prosperous whites owned at least one slave. Free blacks lived near the present Winchester Square in a small colony, and others lived scattered throughout the Springfield area on their own farms. Some prosperous blacks also kept slaves.

The majority of Springfield people were subsistence farmers. However, some crops, such as flax, were raised for trade. Linseed oil was made from its seed, and flax was used to make Irish linen, so it was exported to Ireland. Women also wove flax into towcloth. These items were sent downriver to Newport, Rhode Island, in exchange for wool, molasses, sugar, indigo dye, and tea.

The items exchanged for flax and towcloth were shipped up the Connecticut River from Long Island Sound by flatboats. These flatboats, seventy feet long and twelve feet wide, had twenty square feet of sail to help them move along with any breeze while their crews used long poles to push the boats upstream against the current. At Warehouse Point the goods were unloaded, carted around the Enfield Falls, reloaded on flatboats, and sent upriver. Men living near the Enfield Falls gave up farming as an occupation in order to cart goods around the falls. Others made a living dragging flatboats down the usually shallow falls on their way south.

Logs and lumber were floated down the river loosely or in sixty-foot-by-twelve-foot piloted rafts. There were a number of sawmills in Springfield, especially along the Mill River, catering to this trade. Shad fishing on the Connecticut River was a major local business. Flat-bottomed boats, similar to flatboats, caught, some sources say, up to twenty tons (20,000 fish) in their nets per season.

There were several businesses in Springfield. Zebina Stebbins had a dry goods store on the corner of Ferry Lane and Main Street. He was also overseer of the poor and made coffins for them at a low group rate. He also owned a pottery where he made mugs, pitchers, teapots, and some cups which were glazed and decorated with geometric patterns. He also owned a factory which made rope and another which produced cloth.

Jonathan Dwight advertised in Springfield's first newspaper *The Massachusetts Gazette and General Advertiser,* in 1782 that at his store he had for sale "East India and New England Rum, French Brandy, tea, chocolate, pepper, ginger, and German steel by the hundred or the single bar."

Store goods, though, were usually purchased by barter. Paper money circulated in Springfield during the Revolution, but it was nearly worthless. Most people desired hard money: gold or silver. But hard money was rare before and after the American Revolution. So something farm-made would be exchanged for something in the store. Bushels of corn would be exchanged for sugar, for example.

The Carew house was built between 1798 and 1800 on land bought from Zenas Parsons, the tavern keeper. It stood on the present northeast corner of Carew Street and Main Street. At that time Main Street did not extend into the North End. It curved eastward and into the present Carew Street. If the house were standing today, its front door would face Carew Street. It was two stories high, painted white, and surrounded by a picket fence which was also white. Green blinds covered the windows. Unfortunately the information available about the Carew house is fragmentary. Bits and pieces of description exist in old newspaper accounts of the house, but most are vague and incomplete. A Palladian window, once over the Main Street entrance to the house, is now owned by the Connecticut Valley Historical Museum.

Carew's tannery was located across the street from the front of his house on the town brook. A fine garden was also across the street and next to the tannery. The garden was away from the house to keep the chickens out of it. The chicken coop was near the house during the summer and in a long yellow barn parallel to Main Street during the winter. Between the house and the barn was a string of outbuildings such as the pigpen, the corncrib, and the wagon house. Beyond these buildings was a two-acre meadow which stretched south on the east side of Main Street. The Carew house was torn down in 1894 to make way for a trolley barn.

Colonel John Worthington is Springfield's best-known figure of the Revolutionary War period because he was Springfield's leading citizen and one of western Massachusetts's most powerful figures. Financially and politically he was influential enough to be dubbed one of "the River Gods," the name given to a select group of men who wielded great control over the economy and the politics of western Massachusetts and the Connecticut River Valley.

Colonel Worthington's father, John Worthington, was born in Hatfield and settled in Agawam in 1701. Eventually he bought land in Springfield and became an innholder on Main Street. He also became a community leader and was chosen in time a constable, a surveyor, a militia leader, and a selectman. John Worthington, his son, was born in Springfield in 1719. He attended Harvard, graduated in 1740, and began to practice law in Springfield in 1744. He built an extensive legal practice and was considered one of the finest lawyers in Massachusetts.

In 1748 Worthington was commissioned a colonel in command of the southern Hampshire County militia. As a militia officer, he took part in several campaigns against the French and their Indian allies. He helped to gather troops and supplies in Springfield for campaigns against the enemy.

Worthington's military commission marked his rise to political power in Springfield. He was elected to town offices and served as a selectman and town meeting moderator. He gained colonial positions and was chosen as Springfield's representative to the Massachusetts legislature. He also served on the Governor's Council, an advisory group. Because of his prominence in Massachusetts affairs, he served on a committee to consider the problems of the Stamp Act.

By 1765 Worthington had become one of several colonial leaders whose job it was to keep western Massachusetts loyal to the king of England. Worthington was so successful that it was said he ruled Springfield with a rod of iron. Between 1765 and 1774, while Boston began to agitate more and more for revolution, he kept Springfield loyal to George III.

Springfield was a conservative community—probably because it accepted the opinions of John Worthington. Throughout the early 1770s, Worthington maintained his position as community leader. Yet events were shaping in Boston which would lead to revolution and independence, events which were beyond Worthington's control, events which would for a time remove him from local political power and from statewide power forever.

The Boston Tea Party occurred in 1773. In response Worthington signed a petition assuring the king that the signers would pay a share of the East India Company's bill for the tea dumped into Boston Harbor.

In 1774 Parliament passed several laws in response to the Boston Tea Party. The port of Boston was closed and town meetings in Massachusetts were forbidden. The closing of the port of Boston was meant to punish that town for the tea party. Town meetings were forbidden because the town meeting, particularly Boston's, had become the center of revolutionary talk and activity. A military governor was dispatched to Boston with an army to run the government of Massachusetts.

Springfield's response to all of these events at first seemed mild enough. The town meeting condemned the Intolerable Acts, as the new British laws were called, and argued against any riot or insult to Parliament. Worthington and Jonathan Bliss signed a letter to the new military governor wishing him well in his new position. Yet in the spring of 1774, the Springfield town meeting contracted with three local gunsmiths for twenty guns. Apparently Springfield was changing its mind. John Worthington wrote a letter to the military governor of Massachusetts, advising him that western Massachusetts was in an uproar over the Intolerable Acts.

In August 1774 a mob marched into Springfield beating drums and blowing trumpets. They flew a black flag in front of the courthouse. Those who supported the British, Worthington among them, were forced to swear that they would not hold office under the new Massachusetts government.

In March 1775 it was reported that at Springfield the Courts of Common Pleas and General Sessions of the Peace, were prevented sitting by a large mob, who kept the justices from entering the courthouse, and obliged them, the sheriff, and gentlemen of the bar to desist, with their hats off, from holding any courts.

During the winter of 1775, Massachusetts towns, Springfield among them, were active. Militia companies were organized and a quarter of the men in them were designated minutemen. Powder, guns, blankets, shot, cartridge paper, powder fuses, spades, pickaxes, iron pots, wooden mess bowls, carpenter's tools, molasses, salt fish,

In order to settle the Breck Controversy, Breck altered some of his religious ideas. As was common in the eighteenth century, his alterations were publicly read. Drawing by F. T. Merril from Mason A. Green's Springfield 1636-1886, History of Town and City, *1886; from the author's collection*

raisins, and oatmeal were stockpiled for militia use. In January 1775 the Springfield town meeting appropriated money to buy ammunition for the town's militia, although some leading citizens, particularly Worthington and Bliss, did not approve.

Reverend Stephen Williams, the pastor of the Long-meadow church, kept a diary. "April 20, 1775. This morning as soon as it was light, the drum beat and three guns were fired as an alarm. The story is that some of the [British] troops had marched from Boston to seize some military stores at Lexington or Concord and some men had been killed. . . . The minute-men are gone to town and men are collecting from various parts and we have reason to fear that much mischief is done."

On April 21, 1775, he further wrote in his diary: "This morning at four o'clock another message is come advising that there had been a smart engagement at Concord between the [British] regulars and our people [the militia], and many killed, but we have but an uncertain account. 'Tis said houses are burnt, and women and children killed. More men are collecting and going forth." Sixty Springfield-area men under Captain Andrew Colton marched "from Springfield for the defense of the United Colonies." By the time this force reached Boston, little was happening. So the men turned out to a tavern, returning home tired and somewhat hung over. The American Revolution had finally begun.

Perhaps 150 Springfield men served during the Revolution. The names of most of them are known, as well as how long they served and where. However, little is known about the duties they performed or the battles in which they participated. Most served for short periods of times, some as little as ten days, and others for three, six, or nine months. Most alternated their time in the service with time at home. They came home to plant or harvest crops. After they were sure their families were cared for, they returned to the war.

Judruthan Sanderson, a cooper, was a militiaman at the siege of Boston in 1775. In a letter to his family dated June 29, 1775, Sanderson wrote: "There was a [word omitted] between Charleston and Cambridge and the King's' troops drove our men out of their entrenchments [at the Battle of Bunker Hill] because they had no powder and they have burnt Charlestown and have entrenched on Bunker Hill and our men have entrenched on Winter Hill. . . . We are building a fort in Roxbury and digging a trench across [Boston's]. . .neck." Sanderson was not present at Bunker Hill, but he did serve throughout the war.

Thaddeus Ferre was a fifer throughout the war. He spent three years in the New York and New Jersey area with Washington's army. He may have been with that army when it was driven out of Long Island and New Jersey and almost destroyed by the British in 1777. He may have seen much fighting, but he left no personal account. For years Ferre, playing his fife, rode in Springfield's Fourth of July celebrations. He died in 1847.

Dr. Charles Pynchon, in his late fifties when the Revolution began, joined the militia in 1777 and by 1778 was running a hospital in Springfield for sick or wounded soldiers. He also cared for a number of smallpox cases isolated in a "pest house" in the middle of the Hassocky Marsh.

Joseph Chapin joined the Continental army in 1777. He was twenty-eight years old and five feet four inches tall. He drove a supply wagon for the army. Ebenezer Bliss did garrison duty at Providence, Rhode Island.

A number of Springfield men were garrisoned at Fishkill, New York, a camp north of West Point on the Hudson River. It had several purposes as a military base. It was a supply and troop center for the Continental army, and its location helped Washington maintain control of the Hudson River Valley. If the Hudson River Valley were taken by the British, they could cut New England off from the rest of the colonies and end the Revolution. Other Springfield men helped garrison Fort Ticonderoga, which guarded the northern approaches to the Hudson Valley. Ticonderoga was

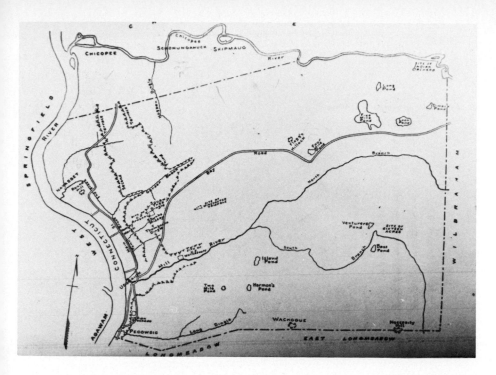

This early twentieth-century map of Springfield shows the principal geographical features and key roads of the town during the seventeenth, eighteenth, and nineteenth centuries. Many of these have been altered or eliminated by twentieth-century construction technology. Drawing by Harry A. Wright, 1900; courtesy of Springfield City Library

a barrier to British invasion from Canada.

Numbers of Springfield men served not only at Fishkill or Ticonderoga but also along the New York frontier. British and Tory-led Indians were making bloody attacks into the river valleys of upstate New York. Casualties were so high among the men who lived in and defended those valleys that a number of Massachusetts troops, Springfield men among them, were sent as replacements.

Nathan Colton served at Fort Herkimer in 1777. The fort was actually a stone house near the settlement of German Flats in the Mohawk Valley. Colton may have witnessed the Indian assault on German Flats which left several dead and the village in ruins in September 1777. Nathan Rowle and David Burt were in General Horatio Gates's Northern army. They may have participated in the Battle of Saratoga, perhaps the most important battle of the Revolution, because it stopped a British invasion from Canada and convinced France to go to war against England as an American ally. After Saratoga, France began to supply America with troops, gold, guns, and the French navy—all of which would make the American Revolution ultimately successful. Nathan Rowle served for one month and three days. He was discharged from service on the day the British army surrendered at Saratoga.

Aaron Steel began the war as a sergeant in Andrew Colton's minuteman detachment. He served later in the Seventh Massachusetts Regiment, Continental army. He did duty on the Pennsylvania frontier against British-led Indians and died of combat wounds at Fort Mifflin, a Continental post on an island in the Delaware River, seven miles below Philadelphia. His family in Springfield was given half his pay until November 1784. He and a number of other Americans died trying unsuccessfully to prevent a British fleet from carrying needed supplies up the Delaware River to British-held Philadelphia.

William White served throughout the Revolution. Like Aaron Steel, he began the war as a sergeant in Colton's company. In 1776 he received a commission. In 1778 he fought Indians on the New York frontier. He was stationed at Fort Alden in Cherry Valley, and on November 11, 1778, he and 450 Continental troops and militia fought off a surprise attack of 800 British and Indians. The commander of the fort was staying at a house outside the fort's walls. The gates of the fort were open. When the raiders struck, the fort's commander was tomahawked before he reached his post. Fourteen of his men were killed in hand-to-hand combat before the gates were closed, and thirty-two inhabitants of the valley also died. Calvin Stevenson of Springfield was also there along with other Springfield-area men. Neither White nor Stevenson left any accounts of what has become known as the Cherry Valley Massacre.

White later participated in retaliatory attacks against Indian villages in western and southwestern New York. In 1780-81 he did garrison duty at West Point and Peekskill. On October 13, 1781, while in the trenches during the siege of Yorktown, Virginia, and now a captain, he was killed by a stray round of British artillery. He had fought in the Revolution from the very beginning to almost the very end. White and a number of friends were standing on the edge of some American trenches observing the British lines when he was killed. Cornwallis's army surrendered six days later, signaling the end of fighting in America and the success of the Revolution.

Once the Revolution began, Springfield supported it. Taxes were raised, supplies were voted, volunteers for the army came forward, private citizens outfitted individual soldiers, and less wealthy people gave up their own blankets and clothes. The people of the town generally supported the war, though there was much grumbling by the early 1780s. When the war was over, the people of Springfield were destitute. Like so many New England towns, they had given much in support of the American Revolution: their wealth, their property, their sons, and their husbands.

On the eve of the American Revolution, Springfield,

though in decline, had unseen potential. The town was strategically located. In the event of a revolutionary war with England, Springfield was a natural location for a military supply center. Springfield was on the Boston Road, which connected the Connecticut shore to Springfield, Boston, and New York City. It was also on the Albany road connecting Albany, New York, with New England. Yet Springfield was still 100 miles from the ocean, and the falls at Enfield, Connecticut, would stop any large ship from navigating up the Connecticut River in an attempt to attack it. The Revolutionary War injected new life into Springfield. In fact, the Revolution and eventually the establishment of a federal armory in Springfield in 1794 guaranteed the survival of the town and its future growth.

The impetus for an armory was provided by Colonel Henry Knox, soon to be in charge of Washington's artillery. In September 1776 he wrote the Continental Congress that he needed capital laboratories, weapons factories a safe distance from the war. He further stated that all kinds of ordnance were needed as well as able artificers, men who could make weapons. He wanted these artificers to produce cannon, wagons, mortars, and howitzers.

Knox had visited Springfield in January 1777 and called it the best place for a laboratory and a cannon foundry in New England. Washington directed Knox to go ahead. Knox informed Congress, writing that the Springfield area had available materials, such as copper and tin, and that preparations for production could begin sooner in Springfield than anywhere else.

Springfield was ready to go into production for the Revolutionary government. A powder mill, sawmills, and gristmills were operating on the Mill River. Wood was readily available. Houses had already been rented, food was cheap, men were already working, and the plain above Springfield—"the hill"—was an excellent site for a laboratory. Congress approved of Knox's choice in February 1777.

Knox's decision in favor of Springfield was probably influenced by the fact that as early as April 1775 Springfield had been producing weapons. In early April, General Gage, the British governor of Massachusetts, sent out British spies to locate colonial supply centers. He sent Lieutenant Colonel Francis Smith and Private John Howe to spy in Worcester and Springfield. Smith, later in April, would command the British troops at Lexington and Concord. At any rate, Smith and Howe, dressed as Yankee workmen looking for gunsmithing jobs, asked a farmer where they would find this kind of work. They were told to report to Springfield to help in gun production.

The first items produced at the laboratory in Springfield were paper cartridges containing powder, of which 7,584 were produced in April 1778. Eventually two operations were performed at the laboratory on Emory Street. Cartridges and fuses were made and filled with powder, and muskets, pistols, and artillery equipment were repaired. Many muskets supplied to America by the French were not in firing condition, so they were sent to Springfield for reconditioning.

The first workshop in Springfield was located near the present intersection of Main and Emory streets in a house rented from Ebenezer Stebbins. It was located there because the ferry crossed the Connecticut River at this point, so military supplies could be moved conveniently across the river north and west. In this house both cartridges and powder were produced. Eventually the Revolutionary government rented or bought a number of buildings throughout the town. A house near the present Dwight Street was rented to produce powder. It blew up at one point, as did a powder-producing house on Emory Street and the powder mill on the Mill River. Making gunpowder was dangerous. Children who filled cartridges commonly lost fingers when the powder accidentally exploded.

Near the present Stockbridge Street, the Revolutionary armory kept horses, and near the State Street side of the Civic Center, a blacksmith shop purchased from Benoni Day shod

Before its development in 1924, Melha Avenue in East Springfield was a good example of an eighteenth-century road: winding, narrow, and of dirt. Courtesy of Springfield City Library

them. A government wheelwright shop operated near the present Park Street and produced wagon wheels. A number of shops like these, producing items for the Revolutionary government, gave Springfield an important role in the war effort.

In April 1777 all of the powder in Boston was sent to Springfield to make cartridges. That same month Springfield became a storage center for war supplies, and twenty-five cases of arms newly arrived in Boston were sent there. All supplies from America's principal ally, France—many cannon, muskets, flints, powder, tents, and lead balls—were sent to Springfield. They were removed from the Atlantic shore because there was a danger that the British might capture them. Springfield then began to supply the whole eastern seaboard, Canada, the frontier, and the navy with military supplies and the Revolutionary War armory also became a recruiting post for the Continental army.

By May 1777 all of the buildings in the vicinity of Emory Street had been rented, and more space was needed. Congress passed a resolution calling for a magazine of 10,000 stands of arms and 200 tons of gunpowder to be located at Springfield. Thomas Dawes, the governmental representative at Springfield, had already drawn up plans for an "elaboratory," the eighteenth century term for a factory, and a magazine for the hill above Springfield. The town meeting leased him some land, and in 1778 the elaboratory, the magazine, and the army barracks were built. Not all work, however, was done on the hill. The Emory Street site was still in operation.

Three men were responsible for the successful operation of the elaboratory. Lieutenant Colonel David Mason was director of the works and responsible for the laboratory. Lieutenant Colonel William Smith was deputy quartermaster general. He organized food and clothing distribution for the men, forage for the horses, and transportation of supplies. Colonel Ezekiel Cheever was commissary of military stores. He stored the supplies and weapons and gave them out on requisition. All three were independent. But they were

ultimately responsible for repulsing the British in the north. They outfitted troops who invaded Canada in 1775-1776, men stationed on the Canadian frontier, and men in the Hudson Valley.

Not much is known of the men who worked at the elaboratory, but in the beginning, at least, they were military men. Men who were skilled in some trade were taken out of the army ranks and sent to Springfield. By 1778, however, many civilians were working at the elaboratory as carpenters, wheelwrights, blacksmiths, and harness markers under military commanders.

Springfield and the elaboratory had some problems getting along together. Springfield was a small, conservative town in 1776. With the establishment of the elaboratory the town was flooded with outsiders who came looking for jobs. There were some foreigners and even deserters from the British army. They had no families; they were new in the town. There were fights in taverns. Livestock, chicken coops, orchards, and gardens were raided. A number of employees were thieves. In the summer of 1778 the town of selectmen petitioned the Massachusetts government that the elaboratory was spending too much money, raising the public debt, increasing the price of food locally, and using public property for private pleasure.

In August 1777 a committee of three was set up to investigate the charges, which were declared unfounded. In 1781 contracts were canceled, surplus material was stored or sold, and the elaboratory rapidly demobilized. By 1781 the war was all but over, even though a peace would not be signed until 1783. Springfield again became a small, decaying town on the Connecticut River. Yet the tradition of Springfield as an excellent site for an armory persisted. In 1794 Washington, remembering the importance of Springfield in the Revolution, made the town the site of the first National Armory. He had also visited the site in 1789 to check the condition of buildings and the military supplies that were stored there.

Springfield and western Massachusetts had whole-

In late March or early April, maple sugar was made. Illustration from Charles H. Barrow's The History of Springfield for the Young, *1923; from the author's collection*

In the early spring sheep were sheared for their wool. Illustration from Charles H. Barrow's The History of Springfield for the Young, *1923; from the author's collection*

Also in the spring the fields were plowed in preparation for planting. Illustration from Charles H. Barrow's The History of Springfield for the Young, *1923; from the author's collection*

In the springtime the fields were cleared of stones brought to the surface by winter erosion. Pen and ink sketch by Carol P. Petell, 1984

During the summer logs were split to make fence rails, which were important to prevent roving livestock from entering cornfields and house gardens. Illustration from Charles H. Barrow's The History of Springfield for the Young, *1923; from the author's collection*

In winter boys trapped rabbits for food. Illustration from Charles H. Barrow's The History of Springfield for the Young, *1923; from the author's collection*

Also in winter, sheep's wool was spun in preparation for making cloth. Pen and ink sketch by Carol P. Petell, 1984

47

The Third Meeting House was built between 1747 and 1750. It stood at the corner of Meeting House Lane (Elm Street) and the Town Street (Main Street). Robert Breck served here as minister for forty-nine years (1736-1785). He preached that non-Christians could go to Heaven if they "acted up to the light they have." Breck was arrested for his ideas by a sheriff from Hartford. He had preached for a time at New London, and the Connecticut authorities wished to keep him from spreading his ideas. He was released after several days and became Springfield's minister. Engraving by Thomas Chubbuck, date unknown; courtesy of Springfield City Library

According to legend, the Old First Church rooster, placed on the Third Meeting House in 1750, was made in London and presented to Massachusetts by a sea captain. The copper bird is five feet tall, four feet long, and weighs forty-nine pounds. Courtesy of Springfield City Library

Middling women" wore long dresses as well as dusters and half-gloves, especially during the winter. From Charles H. Barrow's The History of Springfield for the Young, 1923, artist unknown; from the author's collection

Men wore breeches or full-length pants. Hats were usually worn with the brim down rather than pinned up like a tricorner. From Charles H. Barrow's The History of Springfield for the Young, 1923, artist unknown; from the author's collection

The Carew house, pictured here about 1890, was built by militia captain Joseph Carew in 1800. It stood at the northeast corner of Main and Carew streets. The site is now occupied by a trolley barn renovated by the Peter Pan Bus Lines, formerly the Springfield Street Railway offices and trolley storage barn. In Carew's time Main Street was a dirt path surrounded by meadow, cornfields, and pasture land. Courtesy of Springfield City Library

heartedly supported the American Revolution. Hundreds of western Massachusetts men had served in the army, support of the war had been costly, and high taxes were paid. With the coming of peace, hundreds of western Massachusetts soldiers returned to their homes to discover that their families were heavily in debt. Money was owed for back taxes or to creditors. Massachusetts was experiencing a period of high state debt and great inflation. Hard cash, gold or silver, was not circulating. Only paper money was available, and it was almost valueless. As a consequence, both prices and taxes were high.

To add to the financial difficulties of the times, imprisonment for debt was common. It was not unusual for a creditor to force a debtor into bankruptcy. Under the bankruptcy laws, the first creditor would be paid; others would get nothing. So it was natural for creditors to sue those who owed them money in order to be the first of the creditors to collect. Those in debt were almost automatically sued. All debtor cases were heard before the Court of Common Pleas. Decisions were usually against the debtor, and he would have to pay the court fees. A farmer would be charged seven dollars for the privilege of seeing his farm taken away from him and sold to pay his creditors.

The people of western Massachusetts sought simple, direct answers to explain why times were so bad. They developed a conspiracy theory. Courtroom lawyers, the courts of Common Pleas, and the government of Massachusetts were consciously oppressing them with high legal fees, high taxes, and foreclosures. Several conventions were held in western Massachusetts to seek solutions to these problems, and several were offered. If money was scarce, print more. If lawyers' fees were high, allow anyone of good moral character to act as a lawyer. If the Court of Common Pleas was foreclosing on too many farms, abolish the court.

The first sign of popular unrest occurred in Northampton, where a mob led by Samuel Ely, a graduate of Yale and a former Somers, Connecticut, minister, tried to close the Court of Common Pleas, thinking that this would end bankruptcy foreclosures. Ely was eventually arrested, fined, and sentenced to jail in Springfield. A heavy guard of militia had to escort him from Northampton to the Springfield jail. However, a mob of about 150 men stormed the jail and freed him while most Springfield men were attending the funeral of Longmeadow's minister, Parson Stephen Williams.

In May 1783 the Court of Common Pleas and a second court, the Court of General Sessions, were to meet in Springfield. Sixty men, some armed with clubs, tried to occupy the courthouse on Main Street. There was a street fight. Some men received cracked heads and others bloody noses, but the mob lost. The court sessions were held.

For three years the economic problems in Massachusetts continued. In August 1786 mob violence again broke out. The Court of Common Pleas was not allowed to sit in Northampton. In late September the Massachusetts Supreme Court was to sit in Springfield. A grand jury was to meet with this court. The men who led the mob at Northampton a month earlier were upset. They reasoned that if the jury met, they, the mob leaders, would be charged with treason.

Springfield was tense. General William Shepard of Westfield, a Revolutionary War hero, was appointed by the governor of Massachusetts to command a force of militia at Springfield to protect the court. Shepard's force eventually numbered about 800 men and the mob about 1,200. The mob occupied upper Main Street in the vicinity of present-day Liberty Street, and Shepard's men occupied lower Main Street near the site of the present Civic Center. Both had sentries on the street, each carefully watching the other. Men streamed in from the surrounding countryside, some to join with Shepard, others to join the mob. Springfield itself was divided. Violence was feared at any moment, not only among the outsiders on Main Street, but also within some of Springfield's families.

The mob appeared to have two leaders, Daniel Shays of Pelham and Luke Day of West Springfield. These men did not consider themselves a mob, but called themselves regulators. They felt it was their job to regulate, to set right, the economic and social wrongs which existed in Massachusetts. Many of the men were veterans of the Revolution, and Shays commonly issued orders in a military manner. The men called him General Shays.

The situation in Springfield continued to be tense. Tension was increased by the fact that men changed sides. A militia company, for example, sent to Springfield to help Shepard, joined the ranks of Shays's forces. This situation continued for four days. Shepard held the courthouse, and some of Shays's men wanted to attack, but an attack was never made. Many of Shays's people were not well armed. Shepard, on the other hand, had a well-armed force. He had gone to the arsenal on the hill and borrowed some weapons. He even had a little cannon, called "the government puppy" by the rebels.

Shepard was in a difficult position. He was outnumbered and he feared for the loyalty of his men. Shays was apparently sure of his force because he marched and countermarched them by the courthouse as an insult to Shepard and to show his own strength. The court was open for three days, but no one could be found to serve on the grand jury. The men available were in Shays's or Shepard's forces, or afraid. Finally Shays sent a message to Shepard demanding that he abandon the courthouse. Shepard did. He moved his forces to the arsenal on the hill and quietly dispersed them to their homes.

While Springfield seemed on the verge of civil war, the government of Massachusetts was paralyzed. No one knew how to handle the problems. The senate, made up of conservatives, wanted to suppress the rebels. Part of the house of representatives wanted the rebels pardoned. Nothing was done. In December 1786 Shays and a force of about 350 men raided Springfield and prevented the Court of Common Pleas from sitting. They took possession of the courthouse and no one opposed them. Springfield finally raised a force to oppose Shays after he was gone, but the government in Boston was truly alarmed.

Springfield had been regarded as a government stronghold. As a matter of fact, Springfield had been against many of the changes the regulators wanted to bring about. Now a small force of rebels had entered the town and closed the court. No one had tried to stop them. This time there were no fistfights in the streets.

Something had to be done, yet the state government was powerless. There was no money available to finance an army. The national government was also powerless. Under the Articles of Confederation, all the states had to agree if something was to be done. There was no time to seek total agreement from thirteen individual states. Besides, the Confederation government was heavily in debt itself and had no money with which to raise armies. Finally the businessmen of Boston loaned enough money to the state to raise and equip an army of 4,500 men. These businessmen realized something had to be done. Massachusetts, west of Worcester, seemed to be in a state of revolution.

While funds were being collected in Boston and the call was going out for troops, Shays and his advisors were considering two plans of action. The first involved attacking Boston. This plan was rejected. The second called for capturing the Continental Arsenal at Springfield. This action was more logical because Shays had many men in his forces who were not armed. Once the arsenal was taken, they could be armed, and then possibly Boston could be attacked.

The county that Springfield was a part of, Hampshire, was ordered to raise an army of 1,200 men to be financed by Boston. These men were ordered to gather at Springfield under the command of General Shepard. The rest of the government's forces were to gather at Roxbury, outside of Boston. This force would march to Worcester and westward to Springfield under the command of General Benjamin Lincoln. He was to protect the sitting of the Court of Common Pleas at Worcester and do anything necessary to subdue the rebels to the west.

General Shepard, with about 1,000 militia, took control of the arsenal on State Street hill. He was surrounded. Daniel Shays was in Wilbraham with a force of more than 1,000 men. Luke Day was in West Springfield with a well-drilled, well-trained force of 400. Eli Parsons, a third rebel leader, was in Chicopee, then part of Springfield, with another 400.

Shepard had rebel troops to his east, west, and north. A supply train bringing food, clothing, and rum for his troops was captured in Chicopee by Parsons's force. Shepard was without supplies. He was uncomfortable with his troops because he did not trust them. They wanted pay and rum, and he could give them neither. Some threatened to desert. Shepard turned to the town of Springfield for help. Few would help him, though John Worthington did lend him money. The people of Springfield were either pro-Shays or afraid of him.

Shays sent a message to Day that the attack on the arsenal would occur on January 25, 1787. Shays expected to attack from the east while Day attacked from the west across the frozen Connecticut River, and Parsons from the north. Day never got the message. The messenger stopped in a Springfield tavern for a warm drink of toddy on a cold day and was taken prisoner by men sympathetic to Shepard. He had consumed enough to weaken his resistance.

At four o'clock in the afternoon of January 25, Shays's men, trudging through six inches of snow, marched down the Boston road, now upper State Street, and appeared before the arsenal. Shepard had been warned that Shays's force was on its way. He had divided his force into thirds and deployed them.

There were only three buildings at the arsenal. On the west side of the hill were two barracks or sheds. On the east side of the hill, near the present Magazine Street, was the magazine, full of powder. Shepard had built two forts to protect these buildings. One fort was near the magazine and the other near the barracks. The second one contained cannon. Finally, Shepard also stationed a third of his force on Main Street near the railroad bridge which today crosses the Connecticut River. This force intended to stop Day if he attacked across the frozen river. A mob collected in front of these troops, jeering and perhaps throwing a rock or two, but the mob did not attack. Shays knew he had to take the arsenal quickly because General Lincoln and his forces were marching from Worcester to Springfield. Shays marched his troops by the fort near the magazine and approached the second fort. He stopped approximately where Benton Park, the little park across State Street from the Walnut Street intersection, is today.

In order to stop Shays's advance, Shepard fired some cannon rounds, in warning, to either side of Shays's ranks. Shays did not stop. Shepard then had a howitzer loaded with grapeshot. It was fired directly into the center front of Shays's force. Three men were killed and a fourth died later. Shays's force panicked and fled. Not one musket had been fired on either side. To this day, no one is really sure why a group of combat-experienced troops would panic so quickly, or why Shays doubly exposed his force to Shepard's fire by marching by the first fort to attack the second. In the position in which he placed himself, Shays could have been attacked in the

front, rear, or right flank.

Tradition has it that Day heard the cannon fire in West Springfield and prepared to march. However, Parson Lathrop, the town minister, convinced him that he was wrong and that it might cost him his life. Day remained in West Springfield.

Shepard expected another attack, but Shays had retreated into Chicopee. The following day part of Lincoln's army arrived. Shepard was now reinforced and Shays's Rebellion was drawing to a close. Lincoln's army followed the rebel force up through Amherst and in February finally caught up with its fragments in the midst of a snowstorm. The rebel force was dispersed, and the rebellion was over.

Except for the four men killed, Shays's Rebellion ended happily. The men involved were pardoned. However, the attack on the Springfield arsenal disturbed the government of the United States. As a result a convention was held at Philadelphia in 1787. This convention produced the United States Constitution. The men who attended that convention were clearly aware that during Shays's Rebellion (and similar rebellions in other states) the Confederation government had been powerless and that a band of rebel troops had come very close to capturing the only national arsenal in the country. A new, stronger national government was established principally because of what had happened in Springfield during Shays's Rebellion.

Mrs. Laura B. Carew married Joseph
Carew in 1802. She bore six children and,
according to an unidentifiable 1872
newspaper clipping, was a "remarkably
muscular woman...and did the entire
domestic work for a large household."
Courtesy of Springfield City Library

Captain Joseph Carew owned a tannery
near the present-day corner of Main and
Carew streets. He was a captain during
the War of 1812 and a selectman in the
town of Springfield in the 1820s. He died
in 1843. Courtesy of Springfield City
Library

Justin Lombard built his home in 1787. The last of the eighteenth-century buildings on Main Street, "downtown," it stood opposite the no-longer-existing Hillman Street. In 1893 the property was purchased for $119,000 and demolished to make way for a business block. Lombard had built the house for $1,200. The picture is dated circa 1893. Courtesy of Springfield City Library

Parsons Tavern, now demolished, stood on present-day Court Square in front of the Old First Church. An old elm stood in front of the tavern, allowing just enough room for a wagon to pull up by the tavern's door. No one thought of removing the tree. Courtesy of Springfield City Library

The old courthouse was built on Sanford Street in 1723 and was the scene of a number of confrontations during Shays's Rebellion. By the 1880s it had become a carriage shop, which has since then been demolished. Courtesy of Springfield City Library

Alexander Bliss (1753-1843) was a farmer and a tanner. He owned land in the South End, near present-day Margaret Street. Courtesy of Springfield City Library

Mrs. Abigail Williams Bliss (1768-1807) posed for this picture in 1800. Courtesy of Springfield City Library

Immediately after the battles at Lexington and Concord in April 1775, the news of the outbreak of fighting was carried to western Massachusetts by the ringing of church bells and the arrival of horsemen. The minutemen companies, organized to march at a moment's notice, mustered in larger towns like Springfield and marched to Boston. Sketch by Robert Holcomb; from the author's collection

The Continental powder magazine of 1789 is about all of the Revolutionary period "elaboratory" that survived into the nineteenth century. Artist unknown; courtesy of Springfield City Library

The toll bridge, first built in 1805 and rebuilt several times in the nineteenth century, was closed in August 1922 and replaced by the present Memorial Bridge. This picture was taken circa 1890. Courtesy of Springfield City Library

The interior of the toll bridge presented a view of hand-hewn arches, braces, and posts all held together with thirty-inch spikes of wood, unthreaded key-lock iron bolts, and large iron yokes, which held the posts to the bridge floor. All of this iron was imported from Norway and forged in the valley. Courtesy of Springfield City Library

In this 1827 view of Court Square, the Old First Church stands to the left and the County Courthouse, built in 1823, to the right. The Old First Church was built by Isaac Damon of Northampton, contractor. The sills, beams, posts, and rafters were pre-cut and transported down the Connecticut River from a woodlot in New Hampshire. The woodlot was owned by Levi Chapin. Artist unknown; courtesy of Springfield City Library

General William Shepard's militia faces Daniel Shays's irregulars in front of the town courthouse during Shays's Rebellion. Drawing by F. L. Merrill, from Green's Springfield 1636-1886, History of Town and City; from the author's collection

An 1835 view of Court Square shows a glimpse of Elm Street to the left and West Court Street to the right. Barely visible on Elm Street is the Byers block. It was built in 1835 by James Byers, and, though shortened in length, it still stands today. Engraving by R. O'Brien of a sketch by William S. Elwell; courtesy of Springfield City Library

The Nineteenth Century:
The Growth Of An Industrial City

Chapter Three

This 1839 view of Court Square shows the square's first public fountain. Water piped from State Street hill provided for its continuous operation. The pipes were hollowed wooden logs. Engraving by S. E. Brown of a drawing by John Warner Barber, from John Warner Barber's Historical Collections, *1839; courtesy of Springfield City Library*

In 1662 Hampshire County included three townships: Springfield, Northampton, and Hadley. The area was large, rural, and underpopulated. By 1812 southern Hampshire County was populated enough to create Hampden County, with Springfield the county seat. In Springfield these developments reflected not only population growth but also a gradual industrial development and urbanization which would provide the basis for cityhood in 1852. Other changes in the first quarter of the nineteenth century, though hardly recognized by the town's farmers, reflected Springfield's gradual shift from a static economy based on subsistence agriculture to a more broadly based economy which, to an increasing degree, included both industry and commerce.

In 1805 a private company built a bridge across the Connecticut River. Thought impossible by many, the project was Springfield's most ambitious technological effort at that time and signaled quite dramatically the beginning of a new age. Over 1,200 feet long and thirty feet wide, with five piers and two stone abutments, the toll bridge was an indication of the increasing wagon trade operation between Springfield and upstate New York. The bridge also represented the need for faster and more reliable passage over the river. It augmented a number of ferries which had satisfied local requirements since 1675.

Red and roofless, the wooden bridge was called a "hill and dale." The arch span was the "hill" while the "dale," on end of the pier, was where the hill ended. Each of the spans arched six feet between the piers, improving the bridge's strength and weight capacity but making passage difficult for heavy wagons. Perhaps reflecting community interest and the new bridge's importance, 3,000 people appeared at the dedication. The bridge, in continual use for almost ten years, collapsed in the summer of 1814 when Mr. Bliss of Spring Street was transporting a load of hay from his West Springfield meadow. As he crossed several spans collapsed into the river behind him. Actually, wagon traffic between the Springfield Armory and Albany, a result of the War of 1812, had weakened the bridge and led to its collapse.

The bridge was carefully rebuilt by 1816. Reconstruction was financed by a state-approved lottery offering $13,000 in cash prizes at a time when Springfield's economy was still based primarily on agricultural barter. Piers for the second bridge were constructed of red sandstone transported from Windsor Locks by flatboat. Before the sandstone was put in place, frames of heavy timbers were sunk to the river bottom. These gave form to the rock which was dumped into the river to provide a foundation for the cut sandstone piers. Nine piers, slanted front-upstream to break up the spring ice floes, provided support for a new flat-floored bridge. This second bridge was washed away during a sudden thaw in March 1818. One of the bridge investors, General Dwight, hearing the ice crack and seeing the water rise, attempted to secure a section of the bridge by tying it to a tree. The tree bent, the rope snapped, and the bridge, in pieces, floated off to Hartford.

By 1819 a third new bridge was in place using most of the old bridge's pilings. The final bridge was covered and built of fifteen- to twenty-foot-long hand-hewn pine timbers, many from the previous bridge, pieces of which were salvaged from downriver meadows. The beams were secured by heavy bolts held in place by iron keys. These keys were twisted into slots at the end of each bolt. The builder swore that if this bridge collapsed, he would pay for its reconstruction. The bridge stood until 1922, when the Memorial Bridge replaced it. For 100 years it was a home for bats and rats and was used by suicides, occasional holdup men, and arsonists. The effort expended to keep a bridge over the Connecticut River mirrors its significance to Springfield's growing transportation requirements, a result of the town's gradually changing economy.

During the first quarter of the nineteenth century, Court Square became fixed as the town's center. Before 1821 a large portion of Court Square was the property of Elizabeth Shelton, daughter of Revolutionary-era tavern owner Zenas

This view of the northeast corner of Court Square in 1830 shows the Chapin Tavern, which served the community's first orange soda. Drawing by Charles Copeland, from Moses King's Handbook of Springfield, *1884; from the author's collection*

Parsons. The tavern continued in operation, and near it stood various outbuildings, a hog wallow, and a swamp. Yet by 1820 this unimpressive and seemingly unimportant property became the center of community debate. The issue concerned the location of a new county courthouse, necessary because Springfield had become the seat of the new county. The town's leading business family, the Dwights—who owned a chain of general stores throughout the Connecticut Valley— wanted the courthouse on State Street. In April 1821 a group of Main Street businessmen purchased title to the land from Mrs. Shelton and other claimants and donated the parcel to the new county as the site for the new courthouse. The courthouse, built in 1822, gradually transformed Main Street into the judicial, governmental, commercial, and financial center of the town, a status which has never changed. The formal establishment of a "Court Square" guaranteed the development of the Main Street area before any other town section.

Change was also occurring on the Connecticut River. In the early 1800s fishermen using flatboats and nets caught up to 1,800 shad per day on the river. Until the 1840s fishing was an important local industry. Some of the catch was sold locally and some packed, as in the days of the Pynchons, and shipped out of the area. However, by the 1840s the shad had been fished out and the salmon had disappeared because dams built at Turner's Falls, South Hadley, and Enfield confined them further south below the Massachusetts-Connecticut state line. Shad was so common until that time that it was called "Agawam pork" and sold for less than ten cents a pound.

Before the mid-1820s trade boats were common on the Connecticut River. These flatboats, no larger than ten tons, were propelled on the river by current, sail, and long poles. The boats carried rum and mackerel upriver from Boston, and surplus produce, lumber, fish, and gin from the Springfield area to Long Island Sound. Rum was a major trade item and was shipped in large barrels called hogsheads.

Boatmen, weary from poling, would fill a bottle with water and insert the uncorked nozzle into the bunghole of a hogshead. The water, with a greater specific gravity, would flow into the hogshead while rum flowed out into the bottle. In this manner riverboat men ably supplied themselves with free rum, not only to drink but also to treat shoulder abrasions caused by poling. By the 1830s these boats were replaced by steamboats.

Though change was in process, Springfield remained an agricultural town, little different from other New England towns of the period. There was only limited commercial or industrial development. In 1800, with a population of 2,700, seven sawmills, two gristmills, one fulling and gristmill, a tannery, a paper mill, one duck cloth factory, two distilleries, and several general stores all met primarily local demand. People continued to be subsistence farmers, raising crops and farm animals much as their ancestors had done. Apples were pressed to make cider brandy. Grain seed was broadcast and barrowed and, when grown, harvested with a grain cradle and bolted at the local gristmill. Buckwheat was grown and corn was planted among the potatoes. As late as the 1850s there was land enough near downtown and especially in the outlying neighborhoods—Forest Park, the upper Hill, and Sixteen Acres—to grow hay and raise cattle and sheep. Butter and cheese were cash crops sold to storekeepers and federal armory workers.

Reflecting its agricultural nature, rugged geography, and poor soil, the town was greatly decentralized. Springfield was not one town but many. Clusters of settlement, connected by poorly-developed cart roads, dotted the landscape. The center, one mile north of the Mill River, contained the courthouse and the town hall. Chicopee Parish, part of the town until 1848, contained four mills. Sixteen Acres had a distillery. The Watershops of the infant armory was surrounded by the homes of armory workers, and Indian Orchard had a cotton mill. Each neighborhood, somewhat distinct from the others, also included a number of small

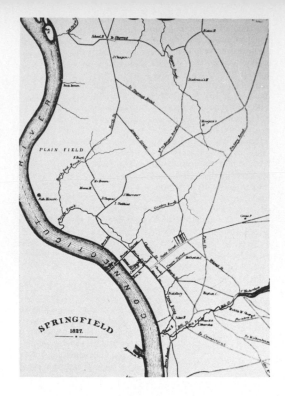

An 1827 map of Springfield shows the sparse development of the riverfront community at that time. Engraving by D. Pelton for Samuel Bowles; courtesy of Springfield City Library

shops, a general store or two, and a poorly maintained school as well as homes and farms.

Each neighborhood cluster was semi-independent and so jealous of the other that a town high school, opened in 1829, closed eleven years later. Geographic isolation had bred political, social, and fiscal divisions. The neighborhoods could not agree concerning school finance, so the school closed. One Indian Orchard mill owner remarked that school interfered with the children's right to work. The town was financially conservative. People rejected the concept of community-wide, tax-financed public improvement. They did not desire to spend public money. In 1828, to further illustrate the point, Springfield built a three-story town hall near the present northeast corner of State and Main streets. Reflecting the town's unwillingness to spend money, the cost of construction was divided into eighths. Therefore the town owned three-eighths of the building and used the second floor for town meetings. The Masons owned one-fourth and claimed the third floor for their meetings. The remaining three-eighths were rented to merchants who operated first-floor shops. By 1857 title to the building became so confused that the city was unable to sell it after a new town hall had been constructed.

Apart from scattered neighborhoods, Springfield's area was open and underdeveloped rather than undeveloped. Elm Street, in the town's center, was a narrow dirt lane in the years before the Civil War. Though the street was long, running to a wharf on the Connecticut River, there were few buildings on it. On the south side, just west of the Main Street intersection, was the "old academy," where boys and girls of the center attended school. Near the school stood the artillery company gun house where the local militia and private military companies gathered for drills. On the north side, and close to the river, stood the hearse storage house, appropriately located since the cemetery, called the "north and south burying ground," was located on either side of the street near the river bank.

Few buildings existed along the east side of Main Street from Bridge Street to the present Chicopee line. A rail fence ran along that side of the street. Confined by the fence, cattle grazed on meadow land that had once been the Hassocky Marsh. Main Street was seasonally mud, dirt, or frozen ruts, sometimes displaying huge puddles wide and deep enough for the homemade rafts of neighborhood boys. In 1790 hogs were forbidden by law to roam the streets. This decision was probably unwise since the hogs had served as garbage collectors, eating the refuse tossed into the town's streets by residents. By 1820 cattle were also forbidden to roam. The town had placed two short, wooden sidewalks on Main Street, and these had to be protected from the casual attacks of the cattle. At this time such side streets as Howard, Bliss, West State, Pynchon, and Vernon were grass and orchard land. There were no buildings over two stories high on Main Street, and most were wooden. Buildings on the east side of the street and to the south of Bridge Street were elevated to avoid flooding. The town brook, covered with removable planking for easy access, flowed under and through some buildings, providing a water supply, natural refrigeration for freshly slaughtered meat, and—when business was slow—a place to fish.

The area of State Street was as little developed as Main Street. Chestnut Street was thickly wooded at present-day Harrison Avenue and Mattoon Street. There was little development between Chestnut and Dwight streets until the 1840s when the town's wealthier people began to build their homes there to get literally above the filth and mud of Main Street. Maple Street extended only to the foot of present-day Central Street. Most of the land between this intersection and the Mill River was pasture for Main Street farms. The present site of Commerce High School, Skunk's Misery Swamp, contained a forest of yellow pines and three or four houses fronting on State Street. The occupants of these houses grew potatoes on terraces which stepped down into the swamp. Roads from the town center, leading out to

Built in 1836 on the south corner of Main and Elm streets, the Chicopee National Bank was founded to meet the needs of a "small class of traders and mechanics." It was demolished in 1884. Courtesy of Springfield City Library

Chicopee, Indian Orchard, Sixteen Acres, East Springfield, or the "X," were flanked by ponds, bogs, swamp, scrub oak, pine woods, and sand flats—valued at ten dollars an acre or less in the early nineteenth century. These other neighborhoods reflected much less development than the town's center.

Despite its appearance, Springfield was in economic and social transition and the federal armory was the root cause, the motivator. The first venture in public manufacturing and one of the first factories in the United States, the armory, in its nineteenth-century production of muskets and rifles, provided Springfield with a self-renewing pool of skilled workmen who had once been tradesmen or farmers. Eventually other industries, seeking machinists and metal workers, were drawn to the area, transforming Springfield from an agricultural town to an industrial, urban city.

By act of Congress in April 1794, a federal armory was established at Springfield. That same year the government rented a small plot of land on the upper State Street hill and moved the Main Street shops of the Revolutionary War period armory to the new site. In 1795 an acre and a half of land was purchased at the intersection of Main and Locust streets, providing for what was called the Lower Watershops. Here iron bars were flattened, cut, and rolled into musket-barrel lengths.

Eventually a Middle Watershops was established near Pine and Mill streets. At this site bayonets were tested by sticking them, musket-mounted, into the shop floor, and then bending the blade from side to side. This was called "taking a set," and it tested the blade's elasticity. If the set was not correct, the pay of the worker who made the bayonet was docked.

The Upper Watershops, bought in 1809 and called Powder Mill Place, was located where the only remaining watershops site is today. There, using a huge water-powered grindstone and polishing machines, workmen smoothed the rough exteriors of newly cut musket barrels. On smaller grinding wheels these men also polished screws, bands, and lock parts.

The sites of the watershops were scattered because the Mill River was an inadequate source of waterpower. Each site needed a location for its own dam. Roswell Lee, superintendent in 1824, wanted to move the armory to the lower falls on the Chicopee River to ensure both waterpower and a consolidated location, but the government rejected his plan. In 1857 the watershops were finally consolidated at their present site. This was possible because in the 1840s steam power began to replace waterpower at the armory. In 1808 Walnut Street, then seventeen feet wide, opened. The street was a sandy path through pine woods. It connected the shops on the hill, where gun parts were finished and assembled, with the shops on the Mill River, where parts were cast and shaped. Parts were transported back and forth in wheelbarrows.

Early armory workers were property-less and migrant. They enlisted for a period of service and took an oath of allegiance. In return they drew wages, food, and a whiskey ration from the government. These men also lived on government property and were totally uninvolved in town affairs. They were noted by a hostile community for raids on local watermelon patches and brawls in local taverns. Springfield had no affection for the armory or the men who worked there. The armory was considered an unnecessary government extravagance, expensive and unproductive, and the workers were viewed as rowdy and criminal. Indeed, armory discipline was lax. Men wrestled and drank while at work. Leaving the shops, armorers walked up Toddy Lane, now Armory Street, to Ingersoll Grove, off present-day Worthington Street. A spring there provided a clean, cold supply of water to mix with their rum. Men, most of whom did unsupervised piecework, also left work to race horses on Walnut Street, to go home to do chores, or to bring their families back to the shops for company.

Two nineteenth-century superintendents, Rosewell Lee and James W. Ripley, were responsible for making the

Elm Street, which runs from Main Street west to the Connecticut River, had become a business street by the mid-1830s. This picture clearly shows the Byers block as it appeared in the 1890s. It stands next to the four-story brick building. Courtesy of Springfield City Library

armory more than an ill-administered "village gun shop." Lee, a gunsmith himself and superintendent from 1812 until his death in 1833, encouraged workers to settle in the area by offering them secure jobs. Lee sought a reliable, permanent, and skilled labor force. Over a period of a generation and more, his goal was achieved.

Encouraging workers to settle permanently in Springfield created social change. Springfield was Congregational, heir to the Puritans, and very conservative. Many of the armory's workers were Methodist, Baptist, Universalist, Episcopal, and Catholic. Springfield disliked outsiders and foreigners. Methodists, arriving by 1815, were viewed as ignorant and lower class. Baptists, present by 1811, were considered overly emotional during their religious services. Catholics, especially Irish Catholics arriving in large numbers by the late 1830s, were intensely disliked because they were papists and viewed as plotting the overthrow of Protestantism. All of these groups were allowed to use the armory chapel, built by Lee, an Episcopalian, for religious services until they were able to acquire or build a meetinghouse or church. Lee was a member of Springfield's Congregationalist First Church but at the time War Department Chapels were Episcopal, so Lee became an Episcopalian. The animosity and suspicion of the native population should not be underestimated. Fear of religious and social diversity was instrumental in keeping the armory out of West Springfield. Originally Congress favored a site on the Agawam River, but Jonathan White, deacon of the Congregational Church, managed to block approval of the site at town meeting. Springfield, therefore, gained the armory by default, since it lacked the political power to keep it out.

Religious diversity in Springfield also bred social and political division to a degree never before experienced in the town. The Congregationalists, especially those of the town center, did not believe in democracy, while the religiously diverse Hill, now the Old Hill and the Watershops neighborhoods, did. The election of Andrew Jackson as president in 1829 led to party spirit and confrontation between the "hill" and the "street." In celebration of Jackson's victory, hickory poles were set up, one at the Watershops and one at the corner of Walnut and State streets. The one at the Watershops was cut down by someone who skated on the still-existent pond so as not to be tracked. The pole at the corner of State and Walnut was, as a result of the first incident, guarded by two men and a dog. Both men were enticed to a nearby grocery for a drink. On return to duty, they found the guard dog well-fed and quiet. The pole had been very quietly "bored down" with an auger. A new pole was put in place and studded with nails to a height of six feet. On Inauguration Day 1830, the Jacksonians wanted house and store windows illuminated with candles in honor of the new president. Edwin Booth, a hat store owner on the hill, refused. The Jacksonians threatened to break his store windows. He threatened to shoot anyone who tried. Fortunately, peace prevailed.

From 1794 until 1841, the armory superintendents were civilians, natives of Massachusetts, and political appointees. During this period Congress required equal rank and authority for the superintendent, the paymaster, and the master armorer. Because of this decentralization of authority, little control was maintained over men or production. James W. Ripley, a major of ordnance, broke with these traditions. To establish his authority Ripley dismissed all the armorers, only gradually hiring them back. He actively sought government funds to modernize the armory. He replaced worn-out waterwheels at the Watershops and decaying buildings on the hill. He supervised the building of new production machinery and the construction of the fence currently surrounding Springfield Technical Community College and the new national park at the old Springfield Armory site. The fence was built to limit the public's casual and thieving access to armory grounds. He transformed the desolate and wild hill location into a beauty spot by trucking in topsoil and planting trees and grass. In modernizing production equipment and

During the 1820s, Charles Stearns, Springfield's master mason and real estate speculator, built one of the few brick blocks in Springfield. The building stood on the southeast corner of State and Main streets. Courtesy of Springfield City Library

establishing worker discipline, Ripley prepared the armory to meet the production needs of the Mexican-American War of 1848, and eventually the Civil War. Changes made during Ripley's tenure allowed for the development of the 1855 rifled musket, the principal Union army weapon of the Civil War.

The armory provided industrial training, inspiring local industrial development and social change. Its operation also encouraged technological innovation. Men of mechanical genius such as Thomas Warner and Thomas Blanchard were attracted to Springfield. Until 1839 each musket produced at the armory was unique. Each metal part was individually worked to fit only a particular weapon. Warner, after visiting several private gun companies and seeing the concept applied, convinced the ordnance department that it would be possible to produce interchangeable gun parts. The idea seems readily acceptable today, but in the 1830s it was still a new idea, and the conservative gunsmiths and workers at the armory were hostile to it. Warner met a government ordnance officer at the Hampden House, a tavern which once stood on the northwest corner of Main and West Court streets, and in a day's time convinced him of the idea's value. By 1842 the armory was producing new model percussion muskets with interchangeable parts.

Thomas Blanchard was the armory's most prolific nineteenth-century inventor. He was born in Sutton, Massachusetts, in 1788. Hard of hearing, Blanchard stuttered, moved slowly, and was never on time. Yet as a child he built mechanical toys, and at thirteen had his own forge. In 1806, at eighteen, he developed a tack-making machine which produced 500 per minute and rang a bell when the required number was made. In 1821 he was hired by the armory to help in the production of weapons, especially to speed up production of gun barrels and stocks. Blanchard had invented a lathe which turned out gun barrels, stocks, and butt plates, replacing thirteen operations in gun production. Called the Eccentric Lathe by the *Springfield Republican,* it could make

any shape in wood, steel, and brass to almost any size. Blanchard's invention was the basis of the machine tool industry.

Blanchard symbolized the industrial age which was descending on Springfield, and he was no fool. On contract with the armory, he received from two to nine cents for each gun produced on his machine. In 1825, for example, the armory produced 13,000 guns. Blanchard also spent $100,000 to protect his patent on the Eccentric Lathe. In 1833, using the machine, he turned busts in cast plaster of senators Henry Clay, Daniel Webster, and John C. Calhoun, placed them in the rotunda of the Capitol, and so impressed the senators that he was given a lifelong patent.

His contribution to industrial development in Springfield did not end with the lathe. In 1826 he built a steam-powered "horseless carriage," called an "idea of great utility" by the *Springfield Republican.* Although no blueprints or pictures of the machine exist today, there is some description available. The machine weighed one-half ton and could carry 1,500 pounds. It consisted of a steam engine mounted on a wheeled platform. Speed was controlled by a series of geared wheels providing low and high forward speeds and a reverse. Blanchard drove his machine up Main Street from Wilcox Street to Carew Street. The fire powering the machine's steam engine went out at Carew Street. It took Blanchard eight hours to rekindle the fire and return home.

Until Blanchard's time the Connecticut River had been a placid north-south trade highway linking Springfield to upriver towns, the Atlantic Ocean, and coastal ports. As Blanchard tinkered with his steam car, others adapted the steam engine for river use. In 1826 the Connecticut Valley Steamboat Company floated the *Barnet,* named for the village in Vermont which the company's investors hoped to reach by way of the Connecticut River. The steamer was a two-engined side-wheeler capable of six miles per hour upstream. Because the Connecticut River is so shallow, the *Barnet* had a flat bottom, was of limited displacement, and

was small. For these features it was nicknamed the "saucepan," a label applied to all early Connecticut River steamboats because of their ungainly appearance. Springfield had several shipyards producing not only traditional flatboats but also steamboats of sixty to seventy tons. In 1827 Thomas Blanchard, drawing royalties from the armory for the work of his lathe, began to build his own steamers, operating them between Barnet, Vermont, and Long Island Sound. His boats were about seventy-five feet long and twenty feet wide, with a two-apartment cabin—one for ladies, one for men—and a promenade deck over all. In 1842 Charles Dickens traveled on one, calling it a "boat for dwarfs" because it was so small and the cabins had such low ceilings. The steamer he journeyed on, the *Massachusetts,* was built in 1831 east of Main Street below Union Street and was pulled on sixteen large iron wheels by 300 men from its place of construction down Main Street and Elm Street to the river. A bottle of rum was broken over its bow at launching.

Travel on these steamers was dangerous. Passengers on some of these early boats had to be towed in barges because there was a danger that the imperfectly designed or built steam engines might explode. The constantly shifting river channel made steamboating difficult, and occasionally passengers had to help push grounded boats off sand bars. The steamboat, though limited in economic impact because of the basic unnavigability of the Connecticut River, did provide Springfield with a swifter connection to the outside world. During the years 1831 to 1845 steamer traffic on the river was brisk, with two boats a day running between Springfield and Hartford. These boats, whether bound downriver for Hartford or for Long Island Sound, carried not only passengers but livestock, liquor, crackers, cheese, and numbers of other items much more conveniently than wagons on the poor roads of the period.

By the 1840s, however, the steamboat business was in decline. By 1839 Springfield and Boston were linked by "rail-road," the Western Railroad, and Springfield became the home office of the line. During the 1830s and 1840s, the town gained two other major trunk lines. One connected Springfield to major Connecticut cities and eventually New York City; the other eventually connected Springfield to cities in northern New England.

Railroad travel in the mid-nineteenth century was primitive by present-day standards. Passenger cars, called "day coaches," were stagecoach bodies bolted onto platform cars. Neither food nor bathroom accommodations was available. Roadbeds were not ballasted and during dry periods passengers choked on the constant dust. Windows were not glazed and passengers breathed the smoke and soot of the wood-burning steam engine. By the late 1840s Springfield was the most important stop in western New England. Rail-related industry, hotels, and restaurants located near the first railroad station, a Quonset-like wooden building located on the west side of Main Street between the present Gridiron and Liberty streets. The Wason Railway Car Company, founded in 1845, produced railroad coaches. Other North End area shops, including the Western's repair shops, produced a variety of railway car parts.

A hotel-restaurant, the Massasoit House, opened on the site of the present-day Paramount Theater, and catered to the food and lodging needs of railroad passengers. Meal time coincided with the railroad schedule; and, as trains pulled into Springfield, a gong was rung to summon the newly-arrived diners. Waffles, fresh Connecticut River shad, and oysters were house specialties over the years. Dining room tables were always covered with linen tablecloths, and each table had a heavy silver candlestick and wax candle for light. Even after the turn of the twentieth century, the Massasoit House continued to use candles instead of electricity. The hotel served meals to Abraham Lincoln; the Prince of Wales, later King Edward VII of England; Daniel Webster, who loved boiled shad served in cream parsley sauce; Charles Dickens; and Jefferson Davis, who became president of the Confederacy. The significance of the Massasoit House does not

lie with its menu or notable guests. The hotel, in its location and operation, was symbolic of the town's increasingly non-agricultural purpose and the economic impact of the railroad. In 1843, when the hotel was first built, the land around it was swampy or agricultural. By the 1860s, as a result of the railroad, the area was built up. The Massasoit House prospered until 1927, when it was replaced by the Paramount Theater which was built into the older structure.

By the late 1840s the process of urbanization and industrialization led to the failure of traditional town government. Until that time, Springfield could continue to be identified as rural and economically static. Until that time the town meeting, controlled essentially by town taxpayers, could administer town needs, which were few. These needs dealt with the condition of town roads, town schools, and town paupers. Little money was spent. The town budget in 1845 was the same as it had been in 1805. Yet this system of government, now 200 years old, was failing due to new pressures not generally recognized or responded to. These pressures were born of industrial development and population growth. In 1790 the population stood at about 1,500; in 1800 it was 2,300; in 1830 it was almost 6,800; by the mid-1840s it was 19,000. The town meeting, well-suited for small numbers of people and unchanging community needs, ceased to function well. In 1849 four political parties represented at town meetings made the election of five selectmen impossible; only three were chosen. In 1851 the town meeting collapsed. Seven factions battled over procedure and agenda. Using a town meeting technique called "evacuation," 1,300 male voters trooped out of the town hall, returning through specially identified doors in order to have their individual votes counted. It took almost two months to choose three selectmen. Political division to this extent was unheard of in the seventeenth and eighteenth centuries. In April 1852 Springfield became a city of 12,000 people, electing a mayor, an eight-member board of aldermen, and an eighteen-member common council. This was without

the 7,000 people of Chicopee which became a separate town in 1848.

Town government failed for a number of reasons. Community needs were increasing. Yet many people in the town failed to see the necessity for sewers, a water supply, or a police department. Neighborhoods jealously blocked improvements of no immediate value to themselves and, even after cityhood, viewed Main Street and the centralization of government there with great suspicion. Only a limited sense of community existed, based upon the cooperative efforts of area farmers in harvesting crops or building barns, not in spending money for sewers, a water supply, or a police force.

The most significant event of the nineteenth century in United States history was the Civil War. Generally the people of Springfield supported Lincoln's war aims: saving the Union and abolishing slavery. Throughout the century Springfield, though involved in the Underground Railroad, accepted the existence of Southern slavery, providing the institution did not expand into other areas of the country. To Springfield people, the issue was not worth civil war. When the English abolitionist George Thompson spoke in Springfield in 1850, his meeting was stormed and he was hanged in effigy at Court Square. This hostile response to an abolitionist may have been due to Thompson's English heritage, not his anti-slavery views. In 1850 Springfield had an anti-English and restless Irish immigrant community, upset over English policies in Ireland and the poor wages paid for the digging of the Holyoke canals. Springfield's attitude changed, however, with Southern secession. People raised to believe that war was romantic and exciting became very patriotic, even happy at its outbreak. They were going to fight to save the Union.

As a result of its extensive rail connections, Springfield experienced the problems and the excitement of Civil War mobilization. Three recruiting camps were located within city limits. There was a camp at Hampden Park, on the road approaching the present North End Bridge. Camp Banks, for bluebloods, was near the Pine Point intersection of Boston

In 1813 the county bought an acre and a half of land on State Street and built a small stone jail. In 1830 a newer, larger jail (the flat-roofed building on the right) was built on the site and was in use until the construction of York Street Jail in 1887. There were twelve cells for men and a number of small apartments for women. After 1887 the building was used as a state armory, and the Harvard-Yale dances were held there after football games at Hampden Park. Classical High School now occupies the site. Courtesy of Springfield City Library

Road and Bay Street. The third, Camp Reed, was located just east of present-day Winchester Square. Except for Camp Banks, these camps were full of mechanics, farmers, and craftsmen from throughout western Massachusetts. Most of them lacked military experience and discipline. Smoking, drinking, following women and girls, they roamed the streets of Springfield, making the citizens nervous. The camp for the Tenth Regiment, Hampden Park, was in some confusion. Men bunked in barns six to a stall, sleeping on bunk beds supplied with "best quality straw." Meals consisted of coffee, boiled rice, and sliced ham and beef, usually poorly prepared. Those who decided not to enlist fought with camp guards whose duty it was to keep everyone in camp until each took the oath of enlistment. Twenty Westfield men refused to take the oath because their officer, democratically elected by militia tradition, had been replaced. Their families also came to protest the government's action. A North Adams man, described as a malcontent, was shorn of hair and whiskers on one side of his face and drummed out of camp. Later, arrested in Springfield for drunkenness, he spent two months in jail.

When the Tenth Regiment mustered in July 1861, the City Guards, a private military regiment, and the city fire department paraded with them before a crowd of almost 5,000 cheering, waving people. In the midst of this carnival atmosphere, the 1,000 men of the Tenth marched to the armory to draw their muskets. The people of Springfield expected a quick, easy victory and were shocked by Union defeats and campaign failures of the early war years. The city may have been more deeply shocked than other communities in the North. Springfield, as a railroad center, saw trainloads of diseased and physically or psychologically crippled soldiers pass through the city on their way home to Massachusetts, New Hampshire, Vermont, and New York cities and towns. Shocked by the condition of these men, Springfield and the Young Men's Christian Commission—soon to become part of the Young Men's Christian Association—established the Soldiers' Rest. By 1864 this privately financed charity had fed,

clothed, changed bandages, and written letters for almost 10,000 returned soldiers, and buried the dead in Springfield Cemetery's Soldier's Rest plot.

Springfield sent about 2,600 men to fight in the Civil War, an average number for a city of fewer than 20,000 people. The wartime experiences of these men were full of bravery, excitement, luck, and death. James D. Orne enlisted as a private in 1861 and mustered out as a captain in 1863. He took part in thirty-six military actions. At the First Battle of Bull Run he was left for dead, unconscious on the field. At Chancellorsville the back of his saddle was shot off. At Gettysburg, his hat was cut in two by a shell fragment. Sergeant Andrew S. Bryant received the Congressional Medal of Honor for his actions at Batchelder's Creek near New Bern, North Carolina. Union ranks had fallen back in the face of an enemy attack. Bryant and his sixteen men held their position and repulsed the attack. Leopold Karpelis, Springfield's first recorded Jewish resident, was a standard-bearer during the Wilderness Campaign in northern Virginia. He received the Congressional Medal of Honor for rallying retreating Union troops who then drove back a Confederate advance. John "Pops" O'Brien, forty-four years old and the father of five, was not lucky. Taken prisoner, he died at infamous Andersonville Prison in 1864. Charles Burt, Springfield's last surviving Civil War veteran, died in 1947 at ninety-nine years of age. He had enlisted in the Union army at sixteen, serving briefly as a drummer.

Spurred by the military contracts of the Civil War, industrial and commercial development made Springfield a prosperous nineteenth-century city. The war fixed the industrial character of the city for almost 100 years. The Wason Railway Car Company, ordinarily a producer of railroad coaches, manufactured gun carriages for the Union army, ultimately employing 1,000 men, up from a pre-war total of 200. Contracts with the company were open-ended, and in 1863 Wason paid a dividend of 44 percent to its investors. Wilkinson and Cummings produced military

In the years before the Civil War it was fashionable for young men to join paramilitary organizations complete with privately designed uniforms. Here the Boston Light Infantry is encamped at Springfield in July 1840. The encampment was on State Street Hill, east of the present Springfield Technical Community College. Courtesy of Springfield City Library

saddles, scabbards, belts, and holsters for the Union cavalry. The shop operated on an eighteen-hour-a-day schedule. D. H. Brigham, clothiers, received a four-month contract for 60,000 military uniforms and appealed in public advertisements for seamstresses. Smith and Wesson produced 2,500 .22 caliber pistols a day. Still the plant was one year behind in orders because the pistol was a popular gift for newly assigned recruits. As a result of war production demands, local companies grew and expanded.

The armory also spurred local prosperity. Prior to the Civil War, however, the armory was in limited operation. There were no funds for improving production equipment, testing weapon designs, buying raw materials, or hiring personnel. As a result, there was little weapons development beyond the 1855 rifled musket; and, though the weapon was obsolete before the war began, the armory refused to experiment with a replacement weapon while war demand was so great. As a result most Civil War production at the armory was of the standard Union army rifle, the 1855 model.

In April 1861 only 504 men worked at the armory, producing 1,200 guns a month. By 1865, the year the war ended, the armory employed 3,200 men and produced 1,000 rifled muskets a day, as well as cannon, cannon ammunition, swords, and bayonets. Armory production continued in the face of problems, such as labor, which lingered from prewar days. Men who were both disciplined and skilled were needed. Smoking, loitering, newspaper reading, tardiness, early quitting, and bribing of inspectors had to be suppressed. Labor pirating stopped when private contractors were forbidden to enter the shops. Armory workers, skilled or unskilled, were subject to the military draft. Money was a problem. In 1864, men averaged two dollars a day in pay. Yet the payroll was, at times, four months late, causing men to leave for other jobs.

In spite of these difficulties armory production was modernized. One hundred and thirteen operations were needed in 1860 to produce one musket. By 1865 production was carefully streamlined. Forty-five parts were produced and assembled in 390 specialized steps. Industry, trade, and job availability were spurred by the armory's wartime production. In 1863 one in four of Springfield's population worked at the armory. The presence of the armory in Springfield encouraged the growth of the small arms industry in the Connecticut Valley, which provided 650,000 non-armory rifles for Civil War use. Yet the benefit of the armory was more than economic. Its presence gave the city pride. The armory was essential to the Union's survival. Springfield residents identified with this crucial role, deriving great national status from the fact that the armory provided weapons for the world's largest army.

By 1864 Springfield contained 31.1 square miles, 142 streets, thirty-nine business blocks, ten banks, five insurance companies, seventeen churches, a city hall, a police court, and a science museum. Most of the population, about 22,000, lived and worked within two miles of Court Square. Most city streets were still unpaved, although intersections were now planked with wood for pedestrians who wished to cross. Crooked, muddy, and lined with hitching posts, Main Street was crowded with horses and horse-drawn vehicles. Cows continued to pasture on the east side of the street, and most buildings, still wooden, were not more than two stories tall. Within this environment people continued to suffer diseases born of poor sanitation and a lack of public health services— diphtheria, typhoid fever, scarlet fever, pneumonia, venereal disease, and smallpox. Those over forty years old suffered from rheumatism, and babies were born at home. A city hospital was not built until 1868.

Life for most continued to be traditional. People lived in wooden frame houses lighted by oil or gas lamps and used coal or wood in their stoves for heat. Flour, apples, and potatoes were sold by the barrel, and beef was still sold in quarters. Regardless of the section of the city, people raised their own cows, poultry, and pigs, though the city govern-

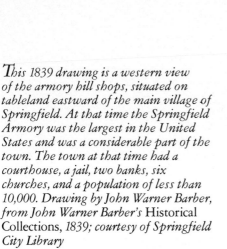

This 1839 drawing is a western view of the armory hill shops, situated on tableland eastward of the main village of Springfield. At that time the Springfield Armory was the largest in the United States and was a considerable part of the town. The town at that time had a courthouse, a jail, two banks, six churches, and a population of less than 10,000. Drawing by John Warner Barber, from John Warner Barber's Historical Collections, *1839; courtesy of Springfield City Library*

ment was thinking of halting these practices. Milk, meat, and fish were supplied by unlicensed peddlers, and farmers supplied produce directly to private homes.

Although the city maintained much of its pre-Civil War life style, it was changing in appearance and shape. Downtown was filling up, and developers, therefore, had to look to other tracts of land. Charles Winchester, who gave his name to Winchester Square and was mayor in 1868-69, bought six acres of land in the present South End and opened up Loring and Lombard streets. In the present Old Hill neighborhood, houses and tenements, many poorly built, filled vacant lots, providing homes for armory workers. Florida, Bay, Hancock, Oak, and Stebbins were built up. Pearl Street had been extended behind the armory and filled with modest houses. In 1864 and after, developers opened Summer Street to the hill, making inroads into old estates, and developed the Mattoon-Elliot Street area. Between 1855 and 1865 the population grew from 13,788 to 22,035, an increase of 65 percent. Seven hundred and fifty houses were built in 1864, and deeds were issued at the rate of 100 a week.

In 1864 Major Henry Alexander, in his inaugural address, called attention to the growing community's newly emergent need for a water supply, a sewage system, schools, fire and police protection, and a horse railroad for public transportation Though he may not have understood the revolutionary nature of his words, Alexander was voicing the city's need for a new community ethic based upon community-wide rather than particularistic needs, a new definition of community born of the city's prosperity and growth. Constructing a new and acceptable public policy concerning city improvements consumed the last twenty-five years of the nineteenth century. It was difficult to separate public need from private right. The old traditions of particularism, frugality, and the concept of limited government persisted.

In 1886 the city of Springfield began to perform functions once thought unnecessary, such as the inspection of milk and the isolation of diseased people. Although begin-

ning to perform new public duties, the city government functioned with difficulty. Because of American dislike of strong centralized government, born of the Revolution, city government was purposely designed to be weak and factional. The city leadership—mayor, common council, and board of aldermen—held loosely defined and decentralized power. The schools, for example, were facing the increasing pressures of urbanization. In 1864 there were 3,808 pupils and seventy teachers in twenty-four schools—about fifty students to each teacher—and truant children infested the streets. One school on State Street had four teachers and 400 pupils, aged five to sixteen. Josiah Hooker, school committee chairman, called for the construction of a three-story, 600-pupil school to replace the older one- and two-room schools. Many people distrusted Hooker's ideas. Large schools were viewed as impersonal and expensive, assigning excessive homework and employing inferior teachers. People living outside the center of town feared that downtown was taking steps to dominate the outlying neighborhoods. The problem was made more difficult by the cumbersome nature of city government. The decisions and reports of the school committee were at the mercy of the common council's standing committee on education. All of the decisions and reports had to be approved by both branches of the council; anyone opposed could stop what was to be done. Further complications arose due to the intense rivalry between the council and the board of aldermen. Yet the community generally supported education, and in 1866 a school designed according to Hooker's ideas was built.

Until the 1840s the residents of Springfield depended upon the Town Brook, wells, and springs for water. Charles Stearns, in the 1840s, organized the Springfield Aqueduct Company. By the late 1850s the company was providing some water to the downtown business center through leaky wooden pipes. The water came from ravines northeast of downtown. Reservoir tanks, called cisterns, were also set up at strategic locations. One located at the intersection of

The area of the Middle Watershops is described in this 1852 account: "The stream which the Ordinance Department has pressed into its service to do its work, is a rivulet that meanders through a winding and romantic valley...." The Watershops were once located on Mill Street near the large intersection at the foot of the Belmont Avenue hill. Engraving from Harper's New Monthly Magazine, *July 1852; courtesy of Springfield City Library*

Worthington and Main streets supplied water to fight fires in that vicinity. As the city began to grow in the 1860s, fear of fire increased. In 1862 the first steam pumper was put into service, marking the end of the volunteer system. Fear of fire and the need for pure drinking water led Daniel Harris, mayor in 1860, to set up a system which pumped water down to Main Street from the hill above. Wells dug to provide water for this experiment caused other wells on the hill to dry up. Harris was not reelected, the Springfield Aqueduct Company was failing, and little was done for almost five years, except for community squabbling over the problem.

In 1864 a shortage of water led to the destruction by fire of Haynes Music Hall, built in 1857 to present "genteel comedies and light farces." A drought was in progress, there was no pressure in the water company's pipes, and the cisterns were empty. Springfield, composed mostly of wooden buildings, was defenseless against fire. Finally in 1865 the Springfield Aqueduct Company signed a contract with Springfield to build a forty-million-gallon reservoir in the present-day Van Horn Park and lay iron pipes to downtown, providing fire safety and water for public buildings. Yet the water problem was not solved until the turn of the twentieth century. By the 1870s the Van Horn Reservoir was too small. A new, larger reservoir was built in Ludlow, but it produced green water and public uproar. Too shallow, the reservoir heated up in spring and summer, producing harmless green algae which sometimes clogged pipes. Finally in 1910 the Little River system was opened. Designed to provide water for a city population of 500,000, it solved Springfield's water supply problems after almost three generations of debate.

Another category of city problems, besides those of education and water supply, was ethnic diversity. Ferry Street, now Liberty, and Railroad Row, now Gridiron Street, became Springfield's most dangerous section. Referred to as a center of rum and rowdyism, it was an Irish slum. Irish immigrants, drawn to western Massachusetts to build the

railroads and dig the canals of Holyoke, lived in an area that was swampy and wet, and which encouraged disease. The streets were lined with saloons and people living in subdivided houses and shacks, raising goats and pigs. There were many street brawls which involved the use of bricks, "Irish confetti," since the North End along Main Street was undergoing a period of construction and the bricks were handy. The area north of the present railroad arch was gang-controlled. The gangs lived in relative harmony, but strangers had to fight gang leaders in order to survive. In the early 1860s there were about fifteen policemen, not uniformed until 1865. The force was far too small to keep peace in a growing, ethnically diverse city. The area above the arch was not calmed until Officer Patrick J. McCallin pacified it in the late 1870s.

Apart from occasional disturbances in ethnic neighborhoods, there was little dislocation as new groups came to live in the city. Many—the Canadian French, the Polish, the Italians—did not speak English; most did not vote or become involved in politics. Blacks made up about 2 percent of the population just after the Civil War and were well and quietly organized in a number of community churches. The opening of Saint Michael's Cathedral in 1866 was celebrated by the city, and Irish participation in the temperance movement gained praise from those who exercised power in the community, the descendants of the Puritans, who were usually Congregationalists. Harmony, however, did not mean lack of discrimination. Irish and black bidders were used at real estate auctions to scare Congregationalists into paying higher prices for property. Harmony existed because the newer ethnic groups in the city were deferential to those holding power.

Industrial development—begun with the Springfield Armory in 1794, spurred by the market-widening development of the railroad and the military needs of the Civil War—continued into the twentieth century. By the 1880s and 1890s a highly diversified and privately developed economy had been brought to maturity. Large factories and small shops produced paper collars, sewing machines, church organs, envelopes, paint and chemicals, iron for buildings and bridges, steam boilers, cigars, candy, crackers, school equipment, soap, and spices. Springfield was considered the perfect place to manufacture because the city could supply both skilled labor and capital, as well as plant sites. Factory buildings existed throughout the city, three, four, and five stories in height, having outside stairways, like inclined planes, leading upward from story to story to the top, each landing a manufactory or more.

Bemis and Call, with a showroom on Taylor Street and shops on the Mill River, had been in business since 1835. By the 1880s, fifty men in those shops produced calipers, compasses, and wrenches. The Springfield Worsted Company on Taylor Street employed fifty workers producing worsted yarns on bobbins, dresser spools or skeins. The Hampden Watch Company at Tyler and Orleans streets employed 400 people in the production of a large line of pocket watches. The R. F. Hawkins Iron Works on Liberty Street—two acres, seven buildings, and more than 150 men—produced wrought-iron bridges, iron viaducts for water, and steam boilers. In a two-story brick building Steere and Turner built cathedral and church organs, including organ woodwork as well as the voicing and the metal pipe making. The Harvey Weyant Brick Manufacturing Yard on Armory Street, established in 1858, produced five million bricks a year on its twenty-five acres of property with clay beds. The Wason Manufacturing Company now was the most extensive manufacturer in Springfield. On sixteen acres of land in the little village of Brightwood, the company produced 100 railroad cars a day in 1883 and employed almost 1,000 men. A. M. Knight and Son, "Plumbers and Sanitary Engineers," located on Main Street, boasted a complete line of pipes, fittings, and washbowls. To a suspicious public they advertised the "sale of water closet apparatus . . . the outgrowth of a practical experience . . . reliable . . . [and] sani-

tary." Samples of the closets, with water, were set up in their store "where they may be seen in operation."

By the 1880s downtown Springfield reflected the city's vitality and prosperity. On Saturday nights, especially in the spring and summer, the entire population seemed to be on the streets, marketing, shopping, or walking merely for recreation and pleasure. At no time in their history were Springfield's people generally more prosperous or optimistic about the city's future.

This is a depiction of the Upper Watershops, which are the present-day Watershops. Pen and ink sketch by S. Van Horn, 1827; courtesy of Springfield City Library

*F*inished bayonets were fixed onto muskets and then set point into the floor to prove their elasticity. If tempered too high, they broke; if too low, they bent. *From* Harper's New Monthly Magazine, *July 1852; courtesy of Springfield City Library*

*I*n the mid-nineteenth century all work done on musket barrels resulted in crookedness. To correct the problem, a worker checked the barrel's straightness by sighting down its interior to a mirror on the floor. The reflection showed the location of the bend, which was struck with a small sledgehammer to straighten it. *From* Harper's New Monthly Magazine, *July 1852; courtesy of Springfield City Library*

*W*orkers assembled muskets at specially designed benches. By 1852 all parts had been standardized. *From* Harper's New Monthly Magazine, *July 1852; courtesy of Springfield City Library*

*I*n 1852, to remove grooves in the exterior finish of a musket barrel, workers used huge grindstones rotating at the then-phenomenal speed of 400 times a minute and held the barrel by an iron rod to a huge, water-cooled, wood-encased grindstone. *From* Harper's New Monthly Magazine, *July 1852; courtesy of Springfield City Library*

The 1852 musket had forty-nine parts. Most of these were formed by forging or "swedging." Dies, "swedges," were brought together around a rod of metal. The upper swedge was hit by a hammer while the lower swedge rested on an anvil. The end result was a rough-shaped musket part. From Harper's New Monthly Magazine, *July 1852; courtesy of Springfield City Library*

In the proving house newly-made gun barrels were tested with gunpowder. Latticework allowed the smoke to escape after bullets were fired into a clay bank in the attached shed at the right. From Harper's New Monthly Magazine, *July 1852; courtesy of Springfield City Library*

The Watershops, built in 1857 and expanded in 1902, has been described as a "slightly medievalized machine shop." The building illustrates the need of nineteenth-century architects to romanticize the features of a factory. The picture is circa 1905. Courtesy of Springfield City Library

In the early nineteenth century Roswell Lee, armory superintendent, built a number of new shops and attempted to control the extensive drinking habits of armory workers. He became superintendent of the armory at Springfield in 1815 and held the office until 1833. He successfully worked at eliminating on-the-job drinking and wrestling at the arsenal. Courtesy of Springfield City Library

James W. Ripley was commandant at the Springfield Armory from 1841 to 1854. Ripley modernized production at the armory and supervised the development of the 1855 rifled musket. By his decision, it became the standard Northern infantry rifle during the Civil War. Courtesy of Springfield City Library

The Baptists were very poor and greatly disliked by area Congregational ministers. By 1811 the Baptists were holding services at the Watershops. In 1821 about fifty members built a meetinghouse at the remote corner of Central Street and Cherry Lane. Courtesy of Springfield City Library

Completed by 1840, Christ Church was located on the north side of State Street east of Dwight. Its Episcopal congregation in 1840 numbered only twenty people. In the early nineteenth century, Colonel Roswell Lee allowed the congregation to hold services at the armory chapel because they were not welcome elsewhere in the town. This building was replaced in 1876 by the present Christ Church Cathedral. Courtesy of Springfield City Library

In 1847 Saint Benedict's Church on Union Street was dedicated. The presence of a Catholic church in Springfield reflected the growth of the city's immigrant Irish population and its increasing power in a strongly anti-Catholic community. Courtesy of Springfield City Library

Thomas Blanchard of Sutton, Massachusetts, was a genius. He invented a lathe capable of turning irregularly shaped forms, and a primitive steam-powered automobile while living in Springfield. Courtesy of Springfield City Library

Thomas Blanchard's Eccentric Lathe provided the basis for modern mass production. Courtesy of Springfield City Library

The Barnet *was the first steamboat to* *reach Springfield from Hartford and the* *first to get as far north on the Connecti-* *cut River as Bellows Falls, Vermont.* *Courtesy of Springfield City Library*

This is an unidentified Connecticut River-type steamboat or "saucepan," a Connecticut Valley term for a flat-bottomed, keel-less boat. Steamboats built by Thomas Blanchard and his competitors most likely resembled this boat, which dates from about 1860. Courtesy of Springfield City Library

The George Bliss house, built in 1824-25, once stood on Chestnut Street where Christ Church Cathedral now stands. It is an example of temple architecture, or Greek Revival style, and was demolished in 1900. Bliss was the first president of the Western Railroad and supervised its construction. He was also community-conscious and offered a tract of land at State and Chestnut streets for a public library. This project was not achieved until 1871. From Springfield Architecture 1800-1900 *by Henry-Russell Hitchcock, 1980; courtesy of Springfield City Library*

Chester W. Chapin, born in 1790, first worked as a farmer. Eventually he became a storekeeper in Springfield and a town tax collector. In 1826 he was a partner in a stagecoach line and became interested in the newly-developing railroads. He eventually became president of the Western Railroad and later the Boston and Albany railroads.

Reflecting his wealth and status, Chapin built this Italianate-style home on the very fashionable Chestnut Street in 1844-45. It is no longer standing, and the site is now occupied by the Fine Arts Museum. *From* Springfield Architecture 1800-1900 *by Henry-Russell Hitchcock, 1980; courtesy of Springfield City Library*

Quarters No. 1, once the home of the armory's commanding officer, was built in 1845-46. Its builder, James W. Ripley, was accused of wasting public money on a "palace." Ripley was disliked because he was not a local man. The house still stands on the grounds of Springfield Technical Community College, the old armory grounds. *Courtesy of Springfield City Library*

In 1840 the George W. Buckland house was built on Church Street, Chicopee. It is an excellent example of Greek Revival architecture, showing simplified Greek temple columns. At the time the house was built, Chicopee was part of Spring-field. *Photo courtesy of John Polak*

These stores on Exchange Street in Chicopee were built in 1840 to house mill workers. Their construction reflects Springfield's and Chicopee's gradual evolution from an agricultural to an industrial economy. *From* Springfield Architecture 1800-1900 *by Henry-Russell Hitchcock, 1980; courtesy of Springfield City Library*

This memorial to Andrew Titus, a prominent realtor in the latter part of the nineteenth century, was cut from a solid piece of marble. The steps are made of East Longmeadow brownstone. The monument stands in the Springfield Cemetery, which was opened in 1839, and exhibits tombstone art dating to the 1600s. The original town cemetery was located on Court Square but was moved to make way for the railroad. From the author's collection

In the Springfield Cemetery there are over 500 stones dating from the seventeenth and eighteenth centuries. This is a close-up of a common gravestone motif of the eighteenth century, the soul effigy. The wings denote the flight of the soul heavenward, and the crown denotes the achievement of salvation. Courtesy of Springfield Cemetery

The Springfield Cemetery became the resting place for Civil War soldiers on their way to New England homes. Dying in Springfield, they were buried in a section of the cemetery called Soldiers' Rest. The memorial statue was added after the war. Courtesy of Springfield Cemetery

(From a Daguerreotype, made in 1842, under the direction of Charles Van Benthuysen.)

AFTERNOON TRAIN BETWEEN ALBANY AND SPRINGFIELD.

STILLMAN WITT, Superintendent at Albany.

THOMAS W. ALLEN, Master Mechanic.   JOHN B. ADAMS, Conductor.

D. S. WOOD, Engineer.   HORACE H. BABCOCK, Ticket Agent.

When the idea of a rail connection between Boston and Albany through Springfield was first proposed, it was considered impossible. One track connected Springfield to Boston by 1839. On these early tracks, fares were paid to the "trainmaster," who carried a whip to keep boys from jumping aboard trains which traveled so slowly that horses could outrun them. Courtesy of Springfield City Library

The Western Railway office, built in 1840, reflected "a calm sure dignity that hardly reflects the exciting business expansion which went on within." The Greek Revival building represented the railroad age, which was to make Springfield a transportation, commercial, and industrial center in the nineteenth century. From Springfield Architecture 1800-1900 *by Henry-Russell Hitchcock, 1980; courtesy of Springfield City Library*

The first railroad depot opened in October 1839 and was a wooden building with "Egyptian-like" towers. Sparks from a wood-burning engine caused a fire which destroyed it in 1851. This second depot opened in 1851 on the same site and was in use until 1889. It was built of red brick and called a "half barrel" because of its shape. Both of these depots were north of Springfield's most famous nineteenth-century hotel-restaurant, the Massasoit House. They stood on the west side of Main Street where the Paramount Theater and the railroad arch are located today. Lithograph by George S. Payne, 1891; courtesy of Springfield City Library

The Massasoit House stood near the southwest corner of Main Street and Railroad Run, now Gridiron Street, next to the railroad station. The railroads, first linking Springfield with the outside world in 1839, made the town the crossroad of western New England. Reflecting this vitality, the hotel expanded several times, adding in the 1850s the four-story brick structure to the left in this picture. Courtesy of Springfield City Library

The Massasoit House interiors show a lavishly furnished bedroom and the vaulted main lobby. Both pictures are evidence of the sumptuous quality of life at the hotel. Courtesy of Springfield City Library

The high school located on West Court Street was built in 1849. In use as a high school until 1874, it was denounced by town residents who saw no need for a school that included cherry-top desks and pine floors. In order to preserve the floors, on entry students had to exchange their shoes for slippers. Although the school was called a palace, it lacked a science lab, a gym, and a library. Today the area is the site of Symphony Hall. Courtesy of Springfield City Library

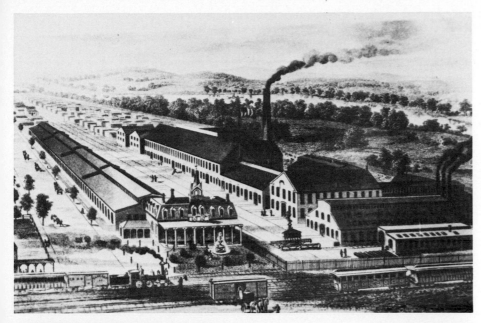

The Wason Manufacturing Company built railroad cars for all American railroad companies and many foreign companies. In the 1870s the company used about 35,000 board-feet of lumber a day, employed 700 workers, and built $1.5 million worth of railroad cars a year. From Moses King's Handbook of Springfield, 1884, artist unknown; from the author's collection

In 1860, during a period of hard times, the Wason Company produced a sleeping car for the Egyptian government at a cost of $300,000. No one knows how the pasha of Egypt heard of a company in Springfield, but his order kept men working at a time when layoffs were common in city industry. Shown here is the Governor Lincoln, the first sleeping car to travel between New York City and Boston. It was built by the Wason Company in the 1870s. Courtesy of Springfield City Library

Sylvanus Adams, looking confident and prosperous, posed for this photograph in 1866. Courtesy of Springfield City Library

An unidentified nineteenth-century wood frame mill building in the South End is a typical representation of early factory construction along the Mill River. Courtesy of Springfield City Library

Located on the northwest corner of Main and Worthington streets, the Wilcox building was a combination of tenements and retail stores. It was the last of the wood frame buildings on Main Street, and it stood in the late nineteenth century when the side streets of Main Street changed from residential to commercial or industrial. Courtesy of Springfield City Library

The alley next to Carlisle's was laid out in 1840 and typified many of Springfield's nineteenth-century streets. It is now the site of the Main Street federal building. The name North Church Avenue commemorates the Old North Church, built in 1848-49, which once stood on the west side of Main Street between Bridge and Worthington streets. The church was founded by Dr. George H. White, a

temperance and anti-slavery advocate at a time when these were unpopular ideas in Springfield. Courtesy of Springfield City Library

Built on Crescent Hill in 1849-50, the John Mills house has been described as one of the finest examples of nineteenth-century Italian villa style in the United States. Mills is standing by the main entrance and his family on the balconies.

Mills was a heavy investor in Springfield real estate and a career politician; as a politician he was described as plump, popular, and honest. In 1848 he helped organize the Free Soil party, an anti-slavery political party that eventually led

to the organization of the Republican Party. From Springfield Architecture, 1800-1900 by Henry-Russell Hitchcock, 1980; courtesy of Springfield City Library

This shows the John Mills house interior as it appeared about 1890. The house still stands at the intersection of Mill and Maple streets. Courtesy of Springfield City Library

This is Aunt Sarah Weiss. Courtesy of Springfield City Library

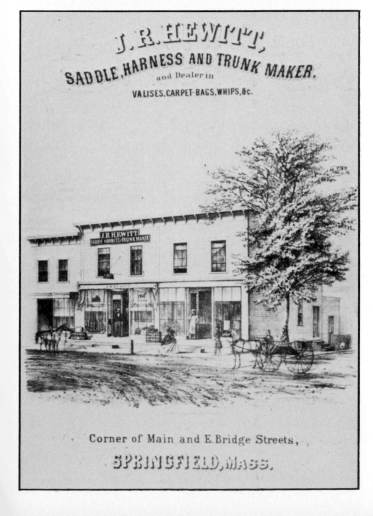

The shop of J. R. Hewitt, harness maker, stood on the northeast corner of Main and Bridge streets between 1853 and 1861. This advertising broadside shows the poor condition of Springfield's Main Street. In the early 1860s the dirt street was cleaned only twice a year. Gangs of men hoed the deep manure/mud up in rows and carted it away in wagons. There were no public sewers, so except for a few private drainpipes which flowed into the town brook, waste was allowed to ooze into the street, making it more damp and filthy. Lithograph by Thomas Chubbuck; courtesy of Springfield City Library

The Homer Foot block, which is no longer standing, was built in 1847 on the southeast corner of State and Main streets. Teams of oxen were used to pull slabs of foundation stone to the site. An iron goods or hardware store, the structure was Springfield's largest commercial building at the time. In 1851 it became the home of Massachusetts Mutual Insurance Company. Courtesy of Springfield City Library

This is Mrs. Charles Miller. Courtesy of Springfield City Library

Samuel Bowles I, 1797-1851, founded the Springfield Republican in 1824. He brought a press up the Connecticut River to Springfield and, with $400 in borrowed money, began his newspaper. Courtesy of Springfield City Library

The Smith and Murray block once occupied the northwest corner of Main and Court streets, which is the present site of the Ban of Boston building. Smith and Murray's was a dry goods store. The block was built in the 1850s and was then a tavern called the Hampden House. Courtesy of Springfield City Library

The Ansel Phelps house was built in 1841 and stands at the northeast corner of Maple and Union streets. Phelps, mayor in the mid-1850s, reflected the new city government's limited sense of purpose. He rejected the idea of a publicly supported city library because city residents were scattered over a large area and might not all share in its use. From Springfield Architecture, 1800-1900, by Henry-Russell Hitchcock, 1980; courtesy of Springfield City Library

Ebenezer Bliss was identified as a "candidate perpetual" for city marshal in the late nineteenth century by Mrs. Charles H. Barrows. She donated this picture to the Springfield City Library in 1925. Courtesy of Springfield City Library

In 1862 Springfield purchased its first steam fire engine, the Monitor, *and quartered it in a building at the corner of Sanford and Market streets. The Civic Center stands there today. The names of the firemen are unknown. Courtesy of Springfield City Library*

This business block, which once stood on the corner of Main and Cypress streets, was built about 1850 for Day and Jobson. It represented the growing business nature of Springfield, with retail businesses replacing the colonial homesteads on Main Street. From Springfield Architecture, 1800-1900, *by Henry-Russell Hitchcock, 1980; courtesy of Springfield City Library*

This Italianate structure, rectangular with tall first-floor windows, was built on Union Street in 1863-64. Photo courtesy of John Polak

The Josiah Gilbert Holland house, built in 1862, was modeled after a Swiss or southern German Alpine cottage. Josiah Gilbert was born in 1819, in Belchertown, Holland. He led a varied life as a medical doctor; a journalist; a school superintendent in Vicksburg, Mississippi; an author of five novels; and a poet. His greatest success, however, was as editor of the Springfield Republican, *a job he began in 1849. The name of his estate, Brightwood, eventually became the name of a section in the city's North End. Photo courtesy of John Polak*

John Brown, abolitionist, was in the wool business in Springfield before the Civil War. While here he helped organize the Gileadites, a group of blacks who promised to fight rather than allow any Springfield black to be returned to slavery. Brown led an unsuccessful raid on the federal arsenal at Harper's Ferry and was hanged for his actions. The raid was part of a plan to arm the slaves of Virginia for a revolt against their masters. It contributed to the outbreak of the Civil War. Sketch by Robert Holcomb; from the author's collection

When the Civil War began, President Lincoln called for volunteers. Springfield became the recruiting center for western Massachusetts; and Hampden Park, which is now a restaurant site near the North End Bridge, became a training camp. Here the Tenth Regiment is on parade. Courtesy of Springfield City Library

For his bravery in battle, Sergeant-Major Andrew Bryant received the Congressional Medal of Honor. Sketch by Robert Holcomb; from the author's collection

Edward K. Wilcox was a captain in the Tenth Massachusetts Volunteers. He was killed in battle. Springfield's Grand Army of the Republic post was named after him. Sketch by Robert Holcomb; from the author's collection

Horace C. Lee was city clerk and treasurer when the Civil War broke out. He was appointed colonel in the locally raised and trained Twenty-ninth Regiment. He was captured by the Confederates and spent a period of time in Libby Prison. Courtesy of Springfield City Library

This picture, one of the earliest views of Main Street, was taken about 1863. The building on the left is the Wilkinson and Cummings shop, supplier of saddlery goods to the Union army. The two-story building with three gabled windows was called the Salamander Building, after a mythical animal able to endure fire without harm, because fires, common in the wooden frame buildings of this time, burned around it, but the building itself never caught fire. Courtesy of Springfield City Library

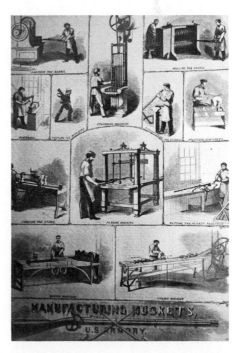

Myron C. Walker posed for this picture on July 15, 1861; however, no record of any Civil War service as a drummer boy appears to exist. Courtesy of Springfield City Library

A series of illustrations published by Harper's Weekly in September 1861 accurately and in detail pictured the Springfield Armory's production line for the 1855 rifled musket, the Union army's principal weapon. Both security and secrecy were lax for much of the Civil War. In 1864 two men from Canada failed in an attempt to blow up the arsenal building, now the Springfield Armory National Historic Site. After that attempt armed groups of private citizens began patrolling the grounds of the armory at night. Courtesy of Springfield City Library
night. Courtesy of Springfield City Library

Commodore Albert G. Clary served in the U.S. Navy during the Civil War and rose to the rank of commodore, retiring in 1876. Courtesy of Springfield City Library

This view of the armory shows the grounds as they appeared in 1862. The building with the flag flying is the West Arsenal. Built in 1807, it was the first permanent building on Armory Square. The arsenal tower was used by riverboat captains and surveyors as a landmark. Courtesy of Springfield City Library

Between 1860 and 1865 the population of Springfield increased from 15,000 to 22,000. Schoolrooms were needed for an additional 1,300 elementary pupils. Temporary schoolrooms were opened in fire stations and a hospital—anywhere space could be occupied for free. The construction of Hooker Street School in 1865 relieved the pressure. This picture was taken circa 1900. Courtesy of Springfield City Library

An 1868 pencil sketch depicts the bridge over the Mill River. At that time the area was called Blake Woods. Today it is the large intersection at the foot of Belmont and Fort Pleasant avenues and Mill Street. The area, rural until the early twentieth century, is now occupied by apartment blocks. Sketch by R. G. Shurtleff; courtesy of Springfield City Library

Railroad Row, now Gridiron Street, was one of the city's busiest streets until the building of the first Union Station on Lyman Street. The old depot discharged all its rail passengers onto this street. Here the hacks, with baggage strapped aboard, awaited passengers. Greundler's Hotel, also known as the Germania Hotel, specialized in the transient trade by offering daily or weekly board. Courtesy of Springfield City Library

Built in 1865 on the northern corner of Main and Pynchon streets, Haynes Music Hall provided Springfield with live theater at a time when most New Englanders considered theater sinful. In order to draw an audience, all of the productions had to be comedies or dramas of "high moral purpose." Courtesy of Springfield City Library

This is a broadside for a two-day performance by General Tom Thumb and his company at Haynes Opera House which replaced the fire-destroyed Music Hall. The program promises "side-splitting comicalities" but also cautions women and children to attend the afternoon show to "thus avoid the crowd and confusion of the evening performance." Courtesy of Springfield City Library

Born in Sudbury, Massachusetts, in 1828, Tilly Haynes began working in a country store at age twelve. At fifteen he peddled "dry goods and Yankee notions." In 1849 he took over a failing clothing store and by 1865 had turned it into a $250,000 business. He built the first theater in Springfield. Courtesy of Springfield City Library

Winchester Square was named after Charles A. Winchester, mayor of Springfield in 1868 and 1869, who died young in 1871. Before 1870, the square was sandy, sparsely populated and the site of a large pond. In 1875 tracks from the downtown depot ran through the square to the Connecticut line. Small industry, residences, and trolley service grew up around them. The fire station was built in 1886 to meet the demand for protection on the hill. The building with the tower is the still-operating Winchester Square fire station. Behind the fire station is the Indian Motorcycle building, now one-third destroyed. For a small amount of money, Prinus Mason sold the city the land that both the fire station and Winchester Park now occupy. Courtesy of Springfield City Library

The Longmeadow Road is an example of the post-Civil War corruption, competition, and community divisions born of American railroad development. Willis Phelps, a Springfield resident and nationally successful railroad builder, proposed in the 1860s to build a rail line connecting Springfield to Hartford and other Connecticut towns through Winchester Square. The plan required the city to invest $150,000. The issue was debated and finally approved in the state legislature. Phelps was accused of blocking an anti-railroad mayoral candidate, rigging a city election, and manipulating the state legislature. All this passion was aroused over a line that was never very significant. Courtesy of Springfield City Library

The Church of the Unity, located next to the Springfield School Department building, was designed in the Gothic style by H. H. Richardson. Richardson used rough-cut local stone and designed the building with a corner tower, a gracefully sloping roof, and large rose windows. The church, finished by 1869, was considered Springfield's most beautiful building. It was demolished in 1962 for a never-built hotel. A new church on Porter Lake Drive was dedicated in 1962. Courtesy of Springfield City Library

Behind the center pulpit in the Church of the Unity were fifty organ pipes for the church organ. These were supported by a bracket of black walnut in maroon and gold, with exquisitely lettered Biblical phrases on bands of blue. Courtesy of Springfield City Library

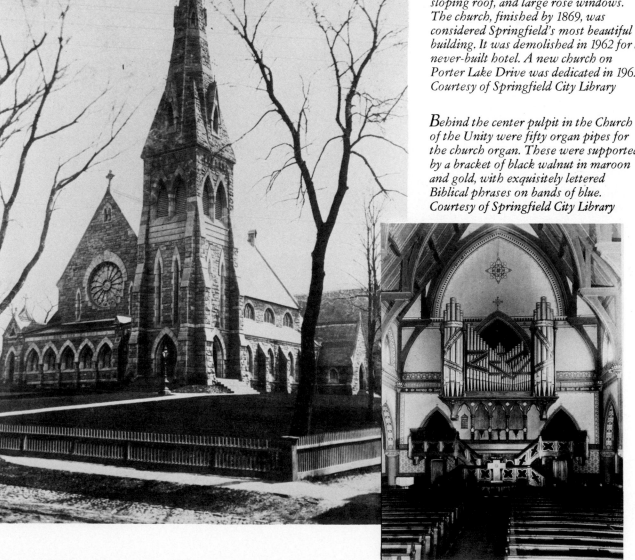

The Springfield Club, begun in 1866, was a factor in the city's social life for thirty years. The club sponsored charity balls, boat races on the Connecticut River, horse-trotting meets, baseball games, and fairs. The fair pictured here at Hampden Park in the North End provided entertainment for about 5,000 people in July 1868. The club encouraged mass entertainment, which helped a rapidly growing, culturally diverse city develop community spirit. From a sketch by Frank Bolles; courtesy of Springfield City Library

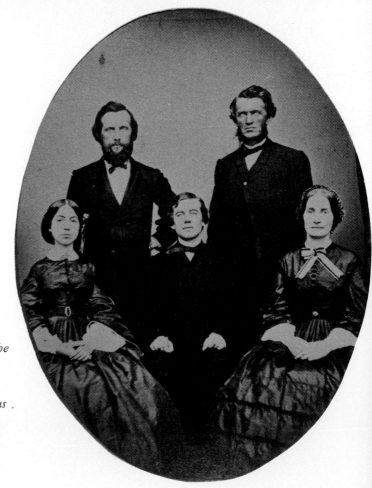

The choir members of the Church of the Unity look very severe in this picture, taken in the 1870s, because shutter speeds on nineteenth-century cameras required subjects to remain stone-still as an exposure was made. Only three people can be identified: far left, Elizabeth Croissette and Mr. Fadd; far right, Miss Briusmade: Courtesy of Springfield City Library

An 1850s print of Court Square shows how much the area had changed since the early nineteenth century. The square was now fenced to protect the grounds from browsing horses. A new city hall, erected in 1854, had been built on the north side, and a new courthouse, designed by H. H. Richardson, which now stands to the east of the present Hall of Justice, was constructed. By 1874 the old courthouse of 1823 had become an Odd Fellows hall. Print by Thomas Chubbock; courtesy of Springfield City Library

This picture of farmers at a Court Square auction was taken in the 1870s. The square was the site for auctions and farmers' markets until the late nineteenth century. Main Street is in the foreground, and Elm Street is to the rear left. *Courtesy of Springfield City Library*

This fountain was built in 1876 by Daniel B. Wesson of the Smith and Wesson Company, as a gift to the city. Today the fountain is still in use on Court Square. The city of Springfield hopes to restore the fountain to its original condition as it appears here. *Courtesy of Springfield City Library*

Born in Maine in 1836, Milton Bradley began in business as a Yankee trader, peddling pens, paper, and envelopes house to house. In 1856 he came to Springfield and began working at the Wason Car Works as a draftsman. In 1860 he bought a press and went into the lithograph business. Because business was slow, he printed the "Checkered Game of Life" and introduced Americans to parlor games. He founded the Milton Bradley Company, which still produces such games as backgammon and Jack Straw, as well as children's school supplies and furniture. *Courtesy of Springfield City Library*

This early twentieth-century photograph depicts men working in the Milton Bradley Company's wood room. Courtesy of Springfield City Library

Pictured here are the people who manufactured Barney and Berry skates in the 1890s. They worked ten hours a day for two to three dollars a day. Courtesy of Springfield City Library

In 1864, at the age of twenty-nine, Everett H. Barney patented a clasp which would easily fasten a skate to a shoe. By the 1870s his factory on Broad Street in the South End was producing clamp-on ice skates and roller skates for a world market. In 1882 he bought 100 acres of land in present-day Forest Park and built Pecousic Villa, which at that time was the most opulent residence in the Connecticut Valley. Barney had great power. For example, since some of his estate was in Longmeadow, he successfully petitioned the state legislature "to restore it to Springfield" so that all of his estate would be within city limits. Courtesy of Springfield City Library

Pecousic, in present-day Forest Park, was the site of a sawmill in 1831, a pistol factory during the Civil War, a papier-mache factory, and a brickyard. By 1894 the Barney mansion, Pecousic Villa, had been constructed. Barney, with an army of gardeners, turned the landscape into a magnificent public garden of exotic plants, lily ponds, graveled paths, and waterfalls which eventually became part of Forest Park. In the foreground is the Warner Pistol Factory, producer of weapons for the Union army; Pecousic Villa is in the background. Courtesy of Springfield City Library

The tomb of Everett H. Barney and his wife, Katherine, and son, George, stands in Forest Park. Courtesy of Springfield City Library

Barney skates were world-famous and won several awards at a number of international expositions. Barney's product was usually cited for originality of design, excellence of quality and workmanship, and ease of operation. Courtesy of Springfield City Library

The Wilkinson and Wight block, at the southeast corner of Main and Taylor streets, was built in the 1860s and is still standing. It housed a paper maker, a boot and shoe dealer, a horse collar manufacturer, and a saddlery. The demand for such products reflected the commercial vitality of the city. Courtesy of Springfield City Library

The Morgan Envelope Company, pictured here in the 1880s, was founded in 1864, operating out of one room. After the Civil War the company landed a huge federal contract for postcards and by the 1880s had built a six-story factory on Harrison Avenue. Today the same firm, known as United States Envelope, occupies a plant in the Memorial Industrial Park. Courtesy of Springfield City Library

The Springfield Institution for Savings was built in 1866-67. The bank used the first floor and rented the rest of the building. To the right and directly behind the bank building is the old town hall built in 1828 by Simon Sanborn. The George and Charles Merriam Company, still headquartered in Springfield, purchased the right to publish Noah Webster's dictionary in 1843 and has been a principal publisher of dictionaries ever since. Courtesy of Springfield City Library

Unidentified Springfield Women's Club members, circa 1900, model clothing styles popular at the time of the Civil War and after. The Women's Club, founded in 1884 and still in existence, was begun as a philanthropic and social organization. It established a summer camp for girls and sponsored plays for public entertainment. Courtesy of Springfield City Library

This detail is from an 1875 map of Springfield. The intersection of State and Main streets is to the right of center in the picture. The city's downtown was extensively developed at this time while South Main Street, now the most densely settled neighborhood in the city, was still relatively undeveloped. Courtesy of Springfield City Library

The great fire of Sunday, May 30, 1875, burned from industrial Taylor Street south-southwest to Vernon, jumping Worthington, Bridge, and Main streets and burning forty-five structures, thirty of them homes. The fire signaled the end of downtown as an area of wood frame buildings and private homes. After 1875 construction was commercial or industrial, and of brick and stone. Courtesy of Springfield City Library

The Waterspout *was an engine belonging to the Springfield Armory and available to Springfield if needed. By 1884, however, engines became* unnecessary because Springfield had 400 hydrants in all sections of the city, eliminating the need for steam pumpers and the rush of volunteers who, after putting out a fire, celebrated with "drunkenness and riot," according to the Springfield Republican. *Courtesy of Springfield City Library*

Looking north from the corner of East Court Street and Main Street, one can see an 1881 view of Main Street including, in order from right to left, the Five Cent Savings Bank, now Community Savings Bank (1876), a considerably altered building; the Springfield Republican building (1878); and the Massachusetts Mutual Block (1867). *Courtesy of Springfield City Library*

A view of Main Street, east side, from Townsley Avenue north to Harrison Avenue, dating from the 1870s. Courtesy of Springfield City Library

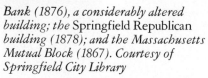

105

This is a south view of Main Street. Bridge Street is on the left. The large tree beyond the seed store marks the present site of the Forum Building, once called the Fuller Block, and the first site of Johnson's Book Store. The picture dates from the 1870s. Courtesy of Springfield City Library

The Fuller block was completed in 1889. Standing on the northeast corner of Main and Bridge streets, it was the most modern building of its time, with above-floor-level bathrooms, air shafts, and passenger elevators. It was called the "crescent block" or "onion building" for its Oriental roof design. The top floor was rented to families and provided one of the best views of the Connecticut Valley. It is now undergoing renovation. Courtesy of Springfield City Library

A 1981 view of the Fuller block, now the Forum Building, shows it shorn of its Oriental ornaments and street-level doorway arches. Courtesy of Springfield City Library

Amos Call, shown here in 1888, was president of the Bemis and Call Hardware and Tool Company of Springfield, a company in operation since 1835 and purported to be the originators of the monkey wrench. Courtesy of Springfield City Library

In 1884 Samuel C. Booth posed with his seventeen-year-old pet cat. Courtesy of Springfield City Library

Malcolm (left) and Homer Harris posed for this picture in 1895. Courtesy of Springfield City Library

A photograph taken in the 1860s shows, from left to right, Charles B. Fisk, Frederick Harris, and W. F. Adams. All became prominent community and business leaders. Courtesy of Springfield City Library

Primus Mason (1817-1892) was a distinguished black philanthropist. He left the bulk of his estate to Mason Hall, a home for elderly men on Union Street. He unsuccessfully searched for gold in California; was a hog farmer in Springfield; a real estate speculator; and an agent in the underground railroad, helping slaves escape to Canada. Courtesy of Springfield City Library

A group of earnest but unknown Victorians posed for this picture in the late 1880s. Courtesy of Springfield City Library

The Masonic Building, today the Ellis Title Building, has stood on the southeast corner of Main and State streets since 1892-93. The Masons used the upper three floors—on the fifth was a 400-seat banquet hall—and rented the rest of the building. Courtesy of Springfield City Library

This view of the southeat corner of Main and State streets was taken in 1981. The brownstone exterior of the Masonic Building has been removed and the street-level storefronts have been remodeled. Developer Gerald Zais has committed $1.4 million to rehabilitate this building by February 1986. The sandstone front will be restored, and the Seth Thomas Clock Tower, also to be restored, will be illuminated. Courtesy of Springfield City Library

The Chicopee National Bank, built in 1889, occupied a building on the south corner of Main and Elm streets. The picture, taken in 1900, shows the Main Street bustle and the street railway work for electric trolley tracks. Courtesy of Springfield City Library

Completed in 1876, Christ Church Cathedral was influenced in its design by the no-longer-standing Church of the Unity. Magnificent in its own right, the church is Romanesque in style. Courtesy of Stanislaus J. Skarzynski

This view of Main Street south from Worthington Street, taken between 1891 and 1893, shows a thriving Victorian city with a typical manure-laden main street. Courtesy of Springfield City Library

A street-level view of the northeast corner of Main and Harrison Avenue, 1889-90, shows a number of buildings. The five-story building, third on the right, was built for the Third National Bank on the south corner of Hillman Street. The facade was ornamental cast iron, a building medium which came into use in the mid nineteenth century. Courtesy of Springfield City Library

Begun as an offshoot of Old First Church in 1841, the South Congregational Church was built in 1876 on Maple Street. Done in simple Gothic style, the interior of the church is magnificently carved in wood and stone, showing plants and animals symbolic of night, morning, spring, summer, and winter, highlighted by two great rose windows. The house to the right of the church is the Samuel Orne mansion built in 1818-19. Orne was a prominent lawyer. The house has since been replaced by an apartment block. Courtesy of Springfield City Library

The 1870s were a period of construction in the city of not only industrial or commercial buildings, but also private residences. Orick H. Greenleaf built a magnificent home on Maple Street, an "English Cottage style" mansion with towers and terraces for the then-staggering sum of $40,000, and called it Riverview. The origins of Forest Park lie in his gift of seventy acres to the city. Courtesy of Springfield City Library

The blizzard of 1888 began on Sunday, March 12, and lasted until the following Wednesday, leaving a snowfall of four to five feet. Although snow drifted two stories high on State Street, the snow melted in three days. This view shows storefronts on Main Street after the sidewalks were hand shoveled. Courtesy of Springfield City Library

Milton A. Clyde, a successful real estate investor and businessman, owned this estate, which stood on Pearl Street. Courtesy of Springfield City Library

This Queen Anne colonial revival mansion is typical of Victorian architecture. It is asymmetrical and massive, sporting exotically-shaped towers, pavilions, and chimneys. Built over a two-year period, 1884-86, the Julius H. Appleton house, still standing on Maple Street, reflected the wealth and ostentation of its paper-company-executive owner. Courtesy of Springfield City Library

John H. Southworth, president of the Southworth Paper Company and of paper mills in South Hadley in the 1880s, was an excellent and aggressive businessman, accumulating a fortune which allowed him to own this house at Round Hill in the North End of Springfield. The hill has since been replaced by a highway interchange. Courtesy of Springfield City Library

The partnership of Horace Smith and Daniel B. Wesson began in 1857 with a work force of about seventy-five men. By 1884 the company had 400 to 500 workers producing 80,000 to 90,000 revolvers a year. In this factory located on Stockbridge Street, now Stockbridge Court Apartments, Smith and Wesson produced weapons for the American military as well as for foreign governments. In 1950 the company moved to a new plant located on what once had been 200 acres of swamp, and employed more than 500 people. This photo of the old factory dates from about 1895. Courtesy of Springfield City Library

The workers at the old Smith and Wesson plant posed for this picture sometime in the 1800s. Courtesy of Springfield City Library

Upper State Street, south side, is pictured here as it appeared in 1874. The street was lined with private homes and estates. There are no longer any private homes between the corner of State and Main streets and Winchester Square. Courtesy of Springfield City Library

The Warwick Cycle Manufacturing Company was organized in 1888 on Hanover Street at the foot of Broad Street in the South End. It became one of the nation's leading producers of safety bicycles, bikes with two equally-sized wheels. During the 1890s biking was the rage and the Springfield Armory closed on weekdays to allow workers to attend bike races at Hampden Park. Courtesy of Springfield City Library

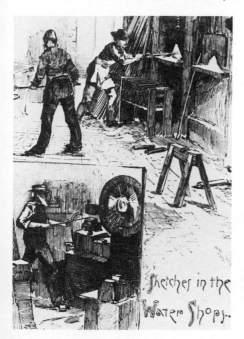

This is an 1873 depiction of armory workers welding and rolling gun barrels and drawing ramrods at the Watershops. From Moses King's Handbook of Springfield, 1884; from author's collection

In the late nineteenth century, rifle parts produced at the Watershops were hauled in wagons such as these to the hill shops between State and Pearl streets for assembly. Courtesy of Springfield City Library

The E. Stebbins Manufacturing Company was located in Brightwood near the Wason Railway Car Company works. A brass works, the company produced castings to order and plumbers' supplies. In 1875 the E. Stebbins Manufacturing Company employed 100 men and was one of the many businesses in Springfield in the post-Civil War era which helped to make the community prosper. Courtesy of the Springfield City Library

Organized in 1880 by Edward H. Phelps on Worthington Street, the Phelps Publishing Company published Good Housekeeping, the New England Homestead, and the Catholic Mirror. Until it closed in the early 1950s, the company also printed and nationally distributed pulp magazines featuring adventure and Western stories, as well as astrology magazines and crossword puzzle books. In 1946 the company printed 4 million magazines a month. Courtesy of Springfield City Library

Located at the northeast corner of Main Street and Worthington, the Brigham and Brown Paper Box Manufacturing Company reflected the growing manufacturing and industrial nature of Springfield during the Civil War and after. Worthington Street, once a side street lined with private homes, was becoming the city's most important industrial-manufacturing area by 1875. Courtesy of Springfield City Library

Catherine Callaghan Toomey came to America about 1900 from Kerry, Ireland, and bore four children. One son became a priest, and the oldest daughter remained at home until both parents passed away, as was the Irish custom. She married at fifty-eight. Photo courtesy of Maureen T. Conway

Samuel Larcom Lewis and Adina Laura Willis Lewis were married in 1885. For a number of years Mr. Lewis ran a cattle ranch in Utah. They were the great-grandparents of Robin Gervicas. Courtesy of Robin L. Gervicas

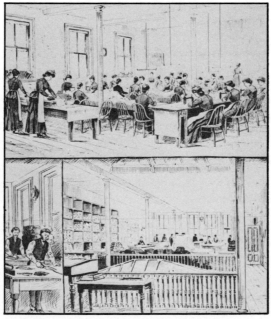

The post-Civil War period was one of great commercial growth. Prosperous merchants opened stores in the new business blocks rising on Main Street. The combination of new buildings and new businesses generated new capital, new investment, and more commercial growth. Represented here is the ready-made clothes business of Theodore L. Haynes Company on Main Street. The year was approximately 1872. Courtesy of Springfield City Library

Springfield's third depot opened on the east side of Main Street in 1889. Built of granite and sandstone, the building was designed by H. H. Richardson, one of the nineteenth century's foremost architects.

The roof-level windows in this 1893 photograph-drawing are sealed because pigeons broke through the originally glassed windows and roosted in the rafters, making walking hazardous on the

concourse below. The building was demolished in the early 1920s and replaced by the present Union Station. Courtesy of Springfield City Library

Classical High School on State Street is part of a school system with 300 years of history and more than 18,000 students, 1,400 teachers, and forty school buildings. The building will be replaced with a modern school building by September 1986. Courtesy of Springfield City Library

Opening in 1898 on State Street, Classical High School, shown here under construction, was the pride of the city. The ceiling in the 800-seat auditorium was paneled with opal-colored and leaded glass. A third-floor conservatory was filled with plants, and next to the conservatory was a revolving dome with a telescope. Courtesy of Springfield City Library

This shows a group of Central High School (now Classical High School) students, circa 1909. Courtesy of Classical High School

This is the Central High School Banjo Club, 1899. Courtesy of Classical High School

A third-year reading class at Tapley School on Bay Street in 1893 pursues its lessons for the camera. Courtesy of Springfield City Library

A gathering of the Bangs family and friends are left to right: Mr. Weiss, Mrs. S. A. Bangs, Ruth Montague, Mable Montague, Mrs. Montague, Elizabeth Bangs, and Mrs. M. E. Bangs. The Bangs family was prominent in area businesses and real estate. Courtesy of Springfield City Library

An unidentified Springfield family poses for a photographer in this undated picture. Courtesy of Springfield City Library

Shown here in 1875 are Mrs. Louisa C. Benton, wife of Col. James G. Benton, and her two grandchildren, Louis B. Suter and J. W. Benton. Col. Benton was commanding officer at the Springfield Armory, 1866 to 1881. Courtesy of Springfield City Library

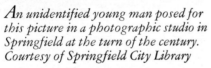

An unidentified young man posed for this picture in a photographic studio in Springfield at the turn of the century. Courtesy of Springfield City Library

This is Anne Rodelia Glover as she appeared in 1895. Courtesy of Springfield City Library

An 1888 picture shows some Springfield baseball players. Seated left to right are: Billie Bull, Bob Granger, and James Hubbard; standing left to right are: Henry Holt, Jim Fletcher, Charlie Warburton, Arthur Town, Reuben Roberts, and Bernie Graves. Mr. Roberts of the Carlisle Hardware Company donated the picture to the city library in 1926. Courtesy of Springfield City Library

William B. Calhoun (1796-1877) *was a prominent city politician in the nineteenth century. He also served in the state legislature and in the national congress. Courtesy of Springfield City Library*

Rev. Samuel G. Buckingham was pastor of South Congregational Church from 1847 to 1894 and later pastor emeritus until his death in 1898. He was also a member of the school committee and a trustee of Williston Academy in Easthampton, Massachusetts. Courtesy of Springfield City Library

The family of Daniel L. Harris posed for this picture in 1880. They are, left to right: Azarrah B., Harriet Otis Harris (Daniel Harris's wife), Lilliace, Sarah, Jeannie, Corinne, Cornelia, Henrietta, D. L. Harris, and Amilia. Daniel Harris was a railroad contractor and president of the Connecticut River Railroad, a line which extended to Vernon, Connecticut, and eventually to Canada. Courtesy of Springfield City Library

It took almost twenty years to raise the money needed to build the old city library located at the corner of State and Chestnut streets. It was replaced at the same location by the present central library building completed in 1912. Courtesy of Springfield City Library

Born in 1832 in New York City, George Walter Vincent Smith began to collect art objects when he was twenty. He made a fortune as a carriage builder and retired at the age of thirty-five to devote himself exclusively to collecting. He and Mrs. Smith traveled, lived abroad from 1882 to 1887, and collected porcelains, bronzes, ceramics, and Oriental armor and weapons. Much of it is now on display in the George Walter Vincent Smith Museum behind the city library on State Street. Courtesy of Springfield City Library

Belle Townsley, pictured here as a young woman, was born in Springfield in 1845. The daughter of a local businessman, she married George Walter Vincent Smith in 1871 and convinced him to settle in Springfield. About fifteen years later, Mr. and Mrs. Smith offered to loan the City Library Association their large art collection and bequeath it to the association after their deaths. The association accepted the offer, land was purchased behind the old city library, and the museum opened in 1895 at the nucleus of the present Quadrangle. The Smith Collection was deeded to the city in 1914. Courtesy of Springfield City Library

The Quadrangle is the little park around which the city library and the various museums are placed. Shown here are the Fine Arts Museum, the Science Museum, and the Connecticut Valley Historical Museum. Courtesy of Stanislaus J. Skarzysnki

The Connecticut Valley Historical Museum at the Quadrangle opened in 1927 and houses a number of collections dealing with Connecticut Valley history as well as collections of glass, pewter, and works of art. Courtesy of Stanislaus J. Skarzysnki

The George Walter Vincent Smith Art Museum houses the private art collection of Belle and G. W. V. Smith. Photo courtesy of Stanislaus J. Skarzynski

The Science Museum opened in 1889 and permanently houses an Indian artifact collection and numerous wild animal specimens, including a cleverly designed African Hall. Photo courtesy of Stanislaus J. Skarzynski

The Museum of Fine Arts, made possible by a bequest from Mr. and Mrs. James Philip Grey, opened on the Quadrangle in 1933. The museum's galleries display a wide array of European, Asian, and American fine arts. Photo courtesy of Stanislaus J. Skarzynski

Before the arch was built, an observer noted that that gates at the Main Street railroad crossing were down and street traffic halted a total of sixty-six times between 11:00 a.m. and 3:00 p.m. on a given day. The picture dates from the 1890s. Courtesy of Springfield City Library

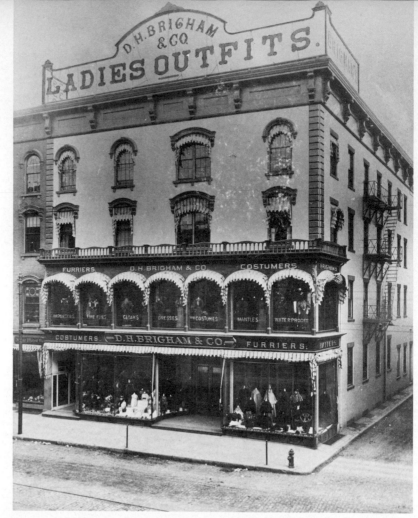

D.H. Brigham opened his clothing business in this building in 1868. By 1898 the store dealt exclusively in women's clothing as shown in these rare interior and show window photos. The business operated until 1969 and is now part of the Marketplace. Courtesy of Leonard R. Skvirsky

In 1869 the state legislature gave its authority for the construction of a new railroad station in Springfield. This decision led to almost twenty years of squabbling over the location of the new depot, whether it should be on the east or west side of Main Street. The station was built on the east side, and squabbles began over the construction of a railroad arch. To compromise, the railroad company, the Boston and Albany, built the bridge, and the city, to increase bridge clearance, excavated the underpass, dropping it four feet below street level. *Courtesy of Springfield City Library*

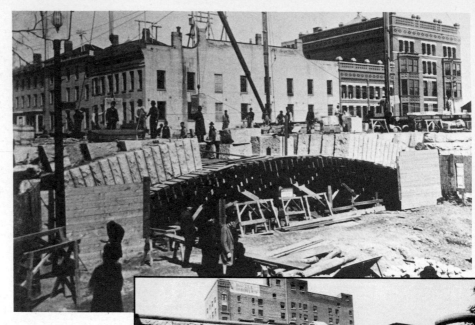

Critics have claimed that the construction of the arch on Main Street in 1890 isolated the North End from downtown, creating a psychological barrier between two once-united neighborhoods. *Courtesy of Stanislaus J. Skarzynski*

The members of the police department in 1904 included patrolmen and superior officers. Patrolmen wore tall helmets, while superior officers wore visored, flat-topped caps. All wore long coats and leather belts, and patrolmen carried clubs fastened to belts on their left sides. The force did not have a chief until 1902. Until that time a politically sensitive city marshal ran a department which in its inventory had two sleighs, one ambulance, one patrol wagon, and a buggy, all horse-drawn. From about 1895 until 1936 the force also had a bicycle squad. *Courtesy of Springfield City Library*

From 1882 until 1897 international bicycle meets with riders from all over the world were held at Hampden Park, now a restaurant site south of the North End Bridge. The park, opened in 1857, was also the site of innumerable fairs, circuses, and "Buffalo Bill's Wild West and Pawnee Bill's Far East Combined Expeditions." Courtesy of Springfield City Library

Shown in this 1885 photo is Robert D. White, who was a prominent member of the Springfield Bicycle Club which hosted racing tournaments in Springfield in the late nineteenth century. Courtesy of Springfield City Library

Wheelmen of the Springfield Bicycle Club posed for this group picture near the corner of Worthington and Main streets about 1893. Courtesy of Springfield City Library

In 1884 this was one of nine wagons distributing Kibbe Candy Company products throughout New England. Courtesy of Springfield City Library

An unidentified soldier from the Spanish-American War of 1898 sports his marksmanship decorations. Courtesy of Springfield City Library

Naval Brigade Company H was the first group of city volunteers to be sent to duty in the Spanish-American War in 1898. Courtesy of Springfield City Library

Springfield men who served in Cuba encountered poor food, poor sanitation, malaria, and Spanish bullets. Six months later they returned to Springfield sick and ragged, disembarking at Union Station. Some were so sick they were taken directly to city hospitals. Others, dazed, were carefully led away by their families, all before a silent crowd of 10,000. This monument, dedicated in 1906, stands on Memorial Square. Courtesy of Stanislaus J. Skarzynski

The Charles A. Bowles house on Mulberry Street was built in 1894 in colonial revival style. Bowles was the second son of Samuel Bowles, the second editor of the Springfield Republican. He was born in New York City in 1861 so that his mother, Mary Schermerhorn, might have the care of New York physicians. Courtesy of John Polak

The Edward F. Pierce house, built in 1897, stands on Longhill Street. The house is colonial revival in style and its architecture incorporated different colonial styles with gambrel-hipped roof, and fan lights over the doorway. Courtesy of John Polak

The E. M. Bugbee Carriage Shop, to the left in the picture, stood at the intersection of Hickory and Hancock streets in the last quarter of the nineteenth century. The picture illustrates the rural nature of the hill neighborhood at that time. Courtesy of Springfield City Library

In the distance beyond the apple orchard stands the home of George Kibbe, a partner in the Kibbe Candy Company. The house still stands on the corner of Worthington and Bowdoin streets in the McKnight Historical District. The picture dates from about 1890. Courtesy of Springfield City Library

George Cook, to the right of the policeman, was Springfield's most notorious "resort proprietor" in the 1890s. A "resort" was a house of prostitution. Courtesy of Springfield City Library

Shown here is Maple Street looking south from the corner of Park Street on the right, circa 1890. Courtesy of Springfield City Library

Built in the California mission style for Eugene A. Dexter in 1897, this house stands on Sumner Avenue. Dexter was a prominent businessman, owning and managing a large bakery on Carew Street in East Springfield. The Dexter Fund now managed by Bay Bank Valley, provides grants three times yearly to public charitable or educational projects for the public good. Photo courtesy of John Polak

Once part of a sandy, white, pine-covered plain east of present-day Springfield Technical Community College, Pine Street by the late nineteenth-early twentieth century had become a fashionable neighborhood. A horse-drawn sleigh disappears on the left side of the picture. Courtesy of Springfield City Library

Thirteen-year-old Harry Montague practices his violin in May 1887. Born in Springfield, Mr. Montague became a baker and eventually lived in Georgia and Florida. Courtesy of Springfield City Library

The Twentieth Century:
The Revival Of A City

Chapter Four

Dr. Cornelius S. Hurlbut, a dentist in Springfield for more than forty years, poses with his wife Mary before the family homestead on Saint James Avenue, about the year 1900. The picture represents Springfield's prosperity and self-satisfaction at the turn of the twentieth century. Courtesy of Springfield City Library

The prosperity of the nineteenth century continued into the twentieth. Springfield remained a manufacturing city as well as a transportation, financial, and commercial center. Symbolic of the city's new urban nature, self-confidence, and vitality, the downtown section thrived with theaters, hotels, stores, banks, offices, factories, and people. No longer a straggling farm village on the Connecticut River, Springfield in 1900 boasted a highly diversified economy and a growing multi-ethnic population of English, Scottish, Irish, black, German, Italian, Polish, French-Canadian, and Chinese, together numbering about 65,000 people.

Yet visitors to the city could still describe it as "a beautiful overgrown New England village," its streets lined with magnificent elms and beautiful single-family homes, all bearing "witness to the intelligent civic pride" of the community's residents. Most city development continued to be within a four- or five-mile radius of Court Square. People walked to work or to downtown entertainment, although inexpensive horse-drawn public transportation was available by 1870 and electric trolleys were operating in 1890. As late as 1949 Springfield, with open land in Sixteen Acres, Forest Park, Pine Point, and East Springfield, was described by author Thornton Burgess as a "successful marriage of country and city" with beautiful unplanned areas such as South Branch Park, which resembled the Maine woods. At the turn of the century most of the land between Winchester Square and the present Memorial Golf Course, the South Branch Park of 1949, was owned by two brothers, Judson and Adoniram Bradley. Judson lived near the North Branch Brook, maintained a farm, and sold butter and eggs at what was, in 1906, called Winchester Park, now Winchester Square. Adoniram lived on Bay Street between Berkshire and Boston roads. He could walk from Winchester Park to his rather isolated home without stepping off his land. Beyond the center there was little development.

In the early twentieth century the city continued its traditional small-town, nineteenth-century entertainments. In the summer, people swam in the Connecticut River. They visited traveling Indian medicine shows in performance on as yet undeveloped downtown lots. At these medicine shows people bought Indian novelties—baskets, bark canoes, bows and arrows; listened to banjo players; and bought Kickapoo Indian Sagwa to cure all internal ills or Kickapoo Indian Oil to cure all external ills. Farmers, as they had done throughout the previous century, gathered at Court Square to sell their farm products. In winter some people skated on the frozen Connecticut River from Holyoke to Enfield, Connecticut, a distance of perhaps twenty miles; went riding in horse-drawn sleighs; or slid down Union Street hill on large sleds called "double rippers."

Although Springfield retained much of its country charm and life style, it had become a city. Downtown Springfield was plagued with air pollution and traffic problems—a result of increased urbanization, industrialization, the absence of zoning regulations, narrow streets, manure-producing horses, and a city government which lacked central authority. Government was based upon the city charter of 1852, which established the position of mayor, a common council, and a board of aldermen. Power was purposely fragmented by the charter: the mayor could veto all legislation, but a two-thirds vote of the councilmen and aldermen could overturn the veto. The mayor also had little power of appointment. Although he headed city government, the mayor's power to manage and to administer was very limited.

City-provided services lacked focus and definition. A street department, for example, had been established and was responsible for building, repairing, and cleaning streets. Between 1887 and 1902 this department experimented with a number of paving materials since no one was sure which was best. Granite blocks, brick, asphalt, and creosoted wood blocks were tried, and there were problems. Wooden pavement, if installed and sealed incorrectly, was slippery and had to be kept sanded or horses would be unable to walk

This is Michael Albano, his wife Christina, and their son Raphael, in 1906. Michael and Christina were the first generation of Albanos in the South End of Springfield. They lived on Gardner Street. Courtesy of Lori J. Perez

on it. Apart from the difficulties of paving experiments gone wrong, the department lacked central authority, and since permits were not yet needed for street work, anyone could rip up a newly-paved street for whatever purpose. A department of engineering had also been established, and by 1902 almost 100 miles of cement and mortar, brick, and clay pipe sewers existed; but these, unfortunately, emptied into the Connecticut River, contributing to a growing pollution problem. A health department also existed, inspecting milk and food, disinfecting streets with formaldehyde and sulphur, and disposing of tubercular animals. This department picked up wet garbage, carted it to the suburbs, Sixteen Acres, and plowed it under, a very unsanitary practice. It would take the city more than half of the twentieth century to define more clearly the mayor's power as well as the authority and the duties of the various city departments, continuing a process begun in the 1850s.

Apart from its park-like appearance, Springfield during the first quarter of the twentieth century experienced a building boom, the result of trolley lines extended beyond the downtown center. It now became possible for people to live several miles from the center and yet be fifteen to twenty minutes away. Land once considered too remote for development was now prime for trolley-stimulated development. Between 1880 and 1930 large tracts of in-city land to the north, south, and east of the old center were developed. In the 1890s, for example, land in the area of Fort Pleasant, Sumner, and Belmont avenues was developed by a number of real estate companies. Land which had been sparsely populated farmland or woods, the location of a one-room schoolhouse, and a small cemetery was subdivided into housing lots on such streets as Cherryvale, Churchill, Garfield, Washington Boulevard, and Washington Road. On these streets Victorian style Queen Anne, classical revival, Tudor, or colonial revival homes, were built.

By 1900 Springfield had shed its early nineteenth-century suspicion of growth and viewed development as both natural and progressive. Architectural landmarks such as the Ely Tavern, dating from the seventeenth century, or the Carew mansion, dating from the early nineteenth century, were briefly mourned and only rarely saved. The land on which these buildings stood was prime land, too valuable to remain undeveloped.

Yet development did not occur without criticism. Page Boulevard, formerly Jennett Avenue, was being developed to provide access to a new manufacturing center in East Springfield. The new center was to be occupied by the Stevens-Duryea Car Company if the city provided street access for a trolley line extension and sewer and water connections. The new street, seventy feet wide, was to pass through the property of B. J. Shaw, cutting through his apple orchard, his grape arbor, thirty-nine pine trees planted by his family, a highly valued plum tree, and his house. He protested loudly, bitterly, and unsuccessfully . The manufacturing center, eventually the location of Springfield's Westinghouse plant, and the new road were built.

During the same period, the Sumner Avenue Extension Company announced plans for the development of 106 acres of land at the remote junction of Sumner Avenue and Allen Street, now East Forest Park. Six hundred and seventy-five house lots and sixteen new streets in alphabetical order and named for well-known automobiles were foreseen. According to plans, six-foot-wide concrete sidewalks, wide tree belts, water mains, and electric lights were to be installed on such streets as Abbott, Benz, Buick, Chalmers, Dayton, Emerson, Fiat, and Ford. Complete development, however, did not occur on these streets until the 1960s. Today homes are being built on land still open between Plumtree and Sumner Avenue Extension.

As Springfield expanded its residential neighborhoods and increased in population by 5,000 to 10,000 every five years, the city continued its existence as an industrial center. Nicknamed the "industrial beehive of Massachusetts," the city had an amazing diversification of industry, being the

These are the Springfield Ice Company delivery wagons on Colton Street near Springfield College, 1890. The company once cut ice from the Watershops Pond for local delivery. Courtesy of George A. Flagg

home of almost 400 manufacturing enterprises within which no particular trade dominated. The armory and other industry demanded metal products and parts, stimulating the operation of several foundries and allied trades in metalwork. Rolls-Royce, located in a Page Boulevard plant, produced metal-over-wood-frame custom bodies in six to eight weeks. With thirteen acres of production space, the Indian Motocycle Company plant at Winchester Square produced a very popular line of motorcycles. American Bosch Magneto needed about 10,000 miles of wire monthly for more than 40,000 company-produced magnetos, one-half of those used in the United States. Bosch also produced starting motors, generators, spark plugs, and battery ignition systems for automobiles. The Diamond Match Company, housed in a new Forest Park plant, produced 3 million boxes of matches a day in 1921. Milton Bradley produced toys, games, and school supplies. This wide industrial and manufacturing base gave great stability to the local economy, generating tax dollars, providing thousands of jobs, and stimulating area retail trade and the transportation industry. Though Springfield was a small city, it was the home of three major department stores—Forbes and Wallace; Meekins, Packard, and Wheat; and Steigers—all thriving because Springfield workers, whose spendable income was above the national average, could afford to buy. The presence of industry, retail trade, and excellent rail connections made Springfield the railroad gateway and the distribution center for New England and New York state, making the city an excellent home base for salesmen. In the 1920s more than 100 trains passed daily through the city.

Even in the midst of the Great Depression in 1938, Springfield people could boast of limited prosperity. Two hundred and ninety-eight manufacturing establishments employed 16,822 men and women in a city of 149,000 people. Depression times, though, were difficult for some. Thousands of Springfield people were underemployed or unemployed. Many worked for reduced wages. Money was scarce and

businesses failed. Meekins, Packard, and Wheat went into bankruptcy and was unable to sell off its third-of-a-million-dollar stock of retail goods, even at half price. The Depression signalled the end of Springfield's industrially-based prosperity, born of Civil War and post-Civil War development. The end came slowly and almost imperceptibly over a period of about fifty years, 1924 to 1975. The decline was so gradual that the community, conditioned to nineteenth-century prosperity and optimism, did not recognize what was happening until the mid-1950s. Industrial decline was a result of several factors: the effect of the Depression; obsolete production items, plants, and equipment; and loss of industry and population to the suburbs or to other sections of the nation. Aging housing stock and manufacturing plants hastened neighborhood decline. All of these problems were further complicated by resistance to needed change.

Industry long identified with community growth and prosperity began to fail. The Kibbe Candy Company, founded in 1843, and thriving in 1926, was foreclosed in 1934, and the building demolished in 1935. In 1926 the company had flourished, employing about 400 people and producing up to 32 million pieces of candy in a five-story plant on Harrison Avenue. Production involved the use of 1 million pounds of chocolate, 2 million pounds of corn syrup, 4.5 million pounds of sugar, and 500,000 pounds of fruit and nuts. The company failed as a result of the Depression. A national market for its product no longer existed.

The Barney and Berry Skate Company, founded in 1864 and located on Broad Street in the South End, had produced ice skates and roller skates for a national market. In 1878 the company employed thirty-five people and produced 80,000 pairs of ice skates. By 1909 up to 150 employees produced 500,000 pairs of ice skates. Everett Barney, one of the founders of Forest Park, had devised a metal-top skate to replace the strap-held skate, thereby "preventing that stagnation of the blood in the foot which was so dangerous." In 1922 the Winchester Repeating Arms Corporation of New

These are the two first-grade classes at Tapley Street School photographed in 1900. Courtesy of George A. Flagg

Haven bought the business, closed it, and moved the plant's machinery to New Haven. In 1935 most of the skate company's industrial complex of twelve factory buildings and other structures between Broad, Hanover, and Elmwood streets were torn down. In 1969 the F. L. Roberts Company purchased the one remaining skate company structure on the corner of Broad Street and West Columbus Avenue, demolished it, and built a gas station-office facility. The Barney and Berry Skate Company failed because, by 1914, the boot skate had replaced the clamp-on skate, and the Barney product was obsolete. Throughout the 1930s the Springfield newspapers were full of articles describing the factories, houses, stores, and sheds being pulled down because the buildings were empty and derelict or because owners wished to reduce their property taxes.

The Kibbe plant, and especially the Barney and Berry plant, built in 1882, typified one of Springfield's twentieth-century industrial problems. Most of Springfield's numerous plants were built during the period from 1880 to 1915. Most of them expanded in a piecemeal fashion as the city and business grew, resulting in a sprawl of multi-story plants designed to meet obsolete needs, making modern production difficult, expensive, and wasteful of space. For instance, the Roller Chain Division of Rexnord, Incorporated, located in the Memorial Industrial Park on Roosevelt Avenue, manufactures a variety of chain which in its most basic form resembles the drive chain on a bicycle. The company located in Springfield in 1878 and expanded over the years as business grew, producing drive chains for the Duryea brothers' first American-made, gasoline-powered automobiles and later for the Indian Motocycle Company. In 1929 the company occupied a mill-type factory building on Plainfield Street in the North End, now the site of the New North School. By the 1950s the building was old and inefficient. The production process, which requires the manufacture of individual components needing assembly, was spread throughout a nineteenth-century building. Chain

components traveled at one time or another from the basement of the building to the second story and back to the main floor for assembly and shipment. Though the plant had been somewhat modernized and expanded, the modern handling, housing, and processing of steel in a multi-level building to produce chain was not competitive within the industry. The floor plan was inefficient. A one-story building was necessary. Obsolete production machinery was also a problem. Although the plant used semi-automatic and foot-pedal equipment, the plant's competition, especially foreign, was far more automated, producing chain at a lower market price. New construction and new machinery solved the problem of obsolescence. In 1970 the company moved into a one-story expandable plant on a 34.5-acre tract in East Springfield's Memorial Industrial Park.

The national defense needs of World War II brought renewed vitality to Springfield industry. In 1939 the Springfield Employment Office had 10,000 applications for jobs on file. By September 1941, almost three months before the United States entered World War II, no male labor was available. The armory expanded from 1,000 to 7,000 workers. Westinghouse, principally a manufacturer of refrigeration and air-conditioning equipment, produced shell fuses and stabilizing equipment for tanks, making it possible for American tanks to move while accurately firing their cannons at the same time. Westinghouse employed 3,000 to 4,000 men, American Bosch almost 4,000, and Indian Motocycle 600 to 800. By 1941 defense production brought industrial employment to levels surpassing those of pre-Depression days. In 1929, 47,700 people worked in city factories. In 1941 the number reached more than 54,000 and Springfield was designated one of thirty-two war production centers.

Yet real industrial growth was minimal in spite of war production. In 1940 Springfield attracted only 6 of 227 new industries in Massachusetts, and only 8 of 127 in-state industrial expansions occurred in the city. A Census Bureau

This is a photo of the Flagg family at Blackberry Hill in 1915. The hill once rose above the intersection of Bay Street and Roosevelt Avenue. The hill is gone—its sand used to make concrete and cinder blocks for the construction of East Springfield. Courtesy of George A. Flagg

study, based on projection of past trends into the future, found that Springfield would eventually lose population or grow very slowly, while at the same time there would be little prospect of rapid postwar economic development. These projections were made in 1943 when the city was experiencing both a labor and a housing shortage, the result of wartime industrial demand.

Springfield, perhaps as an outgrowth of its industrially-based, nineteenth-century prosperity, was very conservative, generally resisting or refusing to accept needed changes. Twice between 1948 and 1959, Springfield voters refused to scrap the nineteenth-century city charter which factionalized government activity in the city. As a result of obsolete government, the city was slow in meeting specific and pressing problems born of industrial decline as they became more intense. Springfield was one of the last of larger American cities to get municipal off-street parking, modern subdivision regulations, traffic administration, urban renewal, highway development, and industrial parks. Problems were further complicated by the city government's refusal to invest money in necessary capital improvements rather than on city services. Between 1955 and 1960 the city experienced the loss of major industry. Indian Motocycle failed; Buxton, Hood, and Package Machinery moved out. Industrial development between the years 1860 and 1930 had spurred commercial, retail, and financial development, drawn people to the city, and stimulated innovation, as in the development of the Duryea automobile of 1893 and the Garand rifle of 1936. The resultant prosperity led to the development of an outstanding educational system both public and private; a fine collection of city museums on the Quadrangle; and excellent recreational facilities such as those found at Forest Park. Loss of industry undermined the tax base which had made these services possible. Springfield needed to develop policies and programs concerning the array of complex problems the city faced. In order to get the community to recognize its deficiencies, dramatic illustrations were nec-

essary. In order to induce Springfield to seek change, the situation had to worsen.

As early as 1935 the area of Congress, Sharon, and Ferry streets was noted for its population decline and vacant stores. Typical of late-nineteenth-century development, the streets of the North End between the Railroad Arch and Memorial Square were narrow and lined with many multi-family dwellings. The streets had not been designed for the automobile and truck traffic they bore. Sewer and water lines were undersized, and little playground space existed for children. By the mid-1950s the problems of North End decay, ignored for almost fifty years, were discussed in a series of newspaper articles. The area was described as sick, transmitting its sickness to other parts of the city. Slum conditions had intensified. In violation of plumbing, gas fitting, and building codes, private homes had been converted into lodging houses. A family of twelve lived in four rooms. Old tenement houses were overcrowded, lacked toilet facilities and hot water, were vermin-infested, and lacked sanitary garbage disposal. Plaster fell from ceilings, wiring was defective, and both lighting and heating were substandard. Yards, hallways, and apartments were piled high with rubble.

Main Street north of the arch was labeled the Barbary Coast, Rum Row, and Gin Lane. There were fifty-one licensed liquor outlets—cafes, package stores, and drugstores—on Main Street above the arch, thirty-seven of them between the arch and Memorial Square. The *Daily News* described the area as the "beer-soaked, butt-sprinkled North End of Springfield." A report financed by the Greater Springfield Council of Churches identified the North End as a classic slum of about 14,000 people. The buildings were in general disrepair, and there was growing unrest and conflict among the many different racial, religious, language, and cultural groups represented by an increasing Spanish-speaking and black population as well as Russians, Greeks, French, Poles, and Syrians. Isolation between groups was increasing, and neighborhood spirit was declining.

This is George F. Flagg. Flagg was a real estate developer who owned large amounts of land in both Pine Point and East Springfield. At heart he was a gentleman farmer, operating a farm in the Pine Point section of the city. Courtesy of George A. Flagg

Neighborhood decay and decline had historical origins. The area above the arch—the North End, Brightwood, and Roundhill—had once been farmland and had been subdivided for residential development. The relocation of the Wason Railway Car Company to Brightwood in the 1870s ended the neighborhood's prestige as a residential area, and poor zoning regulations allowed for the development of spot industry and light manufacturing in the midst of residential housing. As a result of these conditions there was little new investment in the twentieth century, and older dwellings, public buildings, and factories became crowded or outmoded. World War II led to the expansion of industry in the Springfield area and workers flooded the North End seeking housing. There was uncontrolled conversion of property to meet housing needs, accelerating the decline of housing stock.

Sixteen Acres—the area between Boston Road, the Wilbraham town line, Allen Street, Bradley Road, and Breckwood Boulevard—also presented the city with major problems. These problems were not a result of benign neglect and gradually accelerating decay as in the case of the North End. The difficulty in the city's eastern section was rapid urbanization. Sixteen Acres first received its name in the mid-seventeenth century. Rowland Thomas, one of the town's early settlers, received a grant of land totaling sixteen or seventeen acres, west of present-day Parker Street and below the falls of the Mill River. In colonial times the area was sandy and pine-studded. The Mill River was dammed by beavers. Early settlers killed the beaver, drained the beaver ponds, and for more than 200 years farmed the fertile land once covered by those ponds. As late as 1871, Sixteen Acres center contained twelve houses, a gristmill, a blacksmith shop, a ward building for voters, a one-room schoolhouse, two freestone quarries, farms, and a number of summer cottages.

Public transportation, the trolleys, did not reach out to the Acres. Ease of transportation to the rest of the city did not occur until the advent of the automobile in the 1920s. Available and cheap transportation gradually transformed Sixteen Acres into a new residential area, ten new homes a year being built until the Depression years of 1932 to 1935. A small building boom began in 1936, but ended in 1941 with the outbreak of World War II. After the war, Sixteen Acres, zoned for single-family dwellings, entered a period of feverish construction which lasted more than twenty years. By 1960 the neighborhood contained one-third of the city's population of 174,500.

The eastward shift of Springfield's population created problems. In 1960 people who lived in the area of South Branch Parkway lacked paved roads, sewers, and tree belts. Depending on the season, school bus drivers refused to enter certain streets because of their flooded, muddy, or rutted condition. Unpaved streets were private—not maintained by the city—and therefore any necessary repairs to make them passable had to be done by private contractors paid for by street residents. In May 1959 there was a city-wide backlog of more than 900 streets in need of pavement, sewers, and storm drains. Homeowners, because there were no sewers, relied on septic tanks. These in many cases did not function well in the sandy, wet soil of Sixteen Acres. After periods of rain, septic systems, stopped up or with oversaturated tanks and leach fields, would occasionally surface like navy submarines, causing the homeowner to make necessary and expensive repairs. Many yards lacked topsoil for successful lawns, and Sixteen Acres homeowners were humorously referred to as the sovereigns of sandy acres.

Industrial decline, continuing the trend first officially recognized during World War II, continued. The worst industrial shock, however, was the closing of the Springfield Armory in 1968, phasing out gradually during the period 1964-68. Springfield had been the nation's center for small arms research and development. The armory had been in formal operation since the time of the Revolution, providing weapons for that war, the War of 1812, the Mexican-

Shown here is Jessie Jones Flagg in her wedding gown, May 27, 1902. Courtesy of George A. Flagg

American War of 1846-48, the Civil War, the Spanish-American War, World War I, World War II, and the conflicts in Korea and Vietnam. During World War I the armory employed more than 5,000 men and women, producing 1,500 rifles a day. During World War II almost 14,000 workers produced 4 million Garand rifles. Springfield, as it had begun to do during the Civil War, took pride in the location of the national armory. Its presence gave the city a sense of importance few American communities could claim: Springfield identified itself as a key in national defense from the very beginning of the American republic. The closing of the armory broke the city's heart, its collective spirit. The closing did more than psychological damage, however; the armory was Springfield's third largest employer. Its loss signalled the end of Springfield as an industrial or manufacturing city. More than 3,000 jobs disappeared, and 22 million dollars were taken out of the local economy.

The loss of the East Springfield Westinghouse plant, phased out over a period of twelve years, from 1958 to 1970, was part of the same industrial decline. Westinghouse opened in 1915, producing rifles for the Russian army. By 1950 the plant, employing more than 4,600 people or about one of every seven employees in the city, occupied eighteen buildings on a fifty-acre tract, and produced refrigerator compressors, evaporators, iron castings, electric motors, fans, and food mixers.

Apart from the loss of industrially-generated jobs and dollars, Springfield was losing its skilled pool of industrially-trained workers. Men and women, while continuing to live in the Springfield area, began, especially with the closings of major plants, to seek work in the highly industrialized state of Connecticut. Springfield was in danger of losing the skilled people whose presence would draw new and replacement industry to the city. The loss of such industries as the armory and Westinghouse also eliminated the presence of on-the-job training for people wishing to enter the area's skilled labor pool. The pool no longer regenerated itself. Existing business

and industry, especially industry, began to experience skilled labor shortages, a problem which continues.

The city's old center, Main Street, was not immune to the negative twentieth-century forces. Main Street was a victim of core city decentralization. The urbanization of once-remote city neighborhoods, such as Forest Park, East Springfield, and Sixteen Acres, and the development of such suburban neighborhoods as Agawam and East Longmeadow, had drawn population, commerce, and industry to the city's fringes. The development of the automobile after 1900 and government-sponsored highway development after World War II speeded up a process which began in the nineteenth century. Massachusetts Mutual moved from its Main Street site to its present location in 1927. Smith and Wesson moved to its then-new factory in 1950. Between 1950 and 1976, Main Street—once the city's principal shopping and industrial center and provider of almost half of Springfield's tax revenue—had been depleted of most of its businesses except for banks and department stores. The downtown scene was one of vacant lots and empty storefronts in an area once thriving with hotels, stores, offices, theaters, and people. By the mid-1970s the center had lost five movie theaters and had a 20 percent vacancy rate. And in 1976, Forbes and Wallace, the largest department store in the Springfield area and employer of more than 800 people, closed.

By the late 1950s, as shock after shock began to shatter the self-confidence of a once-wealthy and once-industrial New England city, Springfield began actively to seek solutions in order to revitalize what was by 1956 described as a sick city. Many of the solutions are still in progress. Many have caused angry debate and confusion among the city's residents. Some have led to new problems. Yet the solutions which the city found through its citizens, its leadership, and a sometimes very complex process of expedient compromise and false starts resulted in a surprisingly good record of revitalization. Progress at times has been slow; sometimes the resultant changes have met with community suspicion,

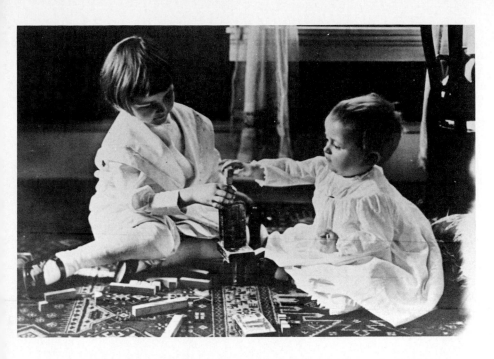

This is George A. Flagg and his brother Frederick playing with blocks in 1912. Courtesy of George A. Flagg

hostility, or indifference. Yet the changes which have occurred over the past twenty-five years have helped the city to survive the twentieth-century decentralization of urban populations and economies, a process which has turned large tracts in many urban areas into wastelands.

In 1959 Springfield voters, three to one, approved the establishment of a Plan A or strong mayor city government. Voters had rejected the weak mayor-bicameral legislature established almost 100 years earlier. The old form of government had obstructed change. Under the new charter the mayor was given considerable power to shape city policy. He could appoint or remove people sitting on various city commissions, agencies, or boards. He submitted the budget to the city council, had the power to approve contracts over $1,000, and was now a member of the school committee. All of these powers, according to the new charter, were to be under the watchdog eye of the city council, a nine-member body elected city-wide. The board of aldermen was abolished. The new city council was also given the power to cut the city budget and approve important appointments, thereby limiting the mayor's authority.

Industrial decline, first apparent in the 1940s, continued into the 1950s. Springfield faced a major problem: the loss of industrial plants to the suburbs or to the South. Plants were being lost to carefully engineered sites where facilities and services were conveniently offered in one-story garden-like settings. The city offered little competition to these attractions. Springfield had a very limited amount of available industrial land. By 1958 community leaders began to recognize the need to attract industry, something the city had never before found it necessary to do.

Debate over the establishment of an industrial park was fueled by events at the city's East Springfield Westinghouse plant. The company was preparing to leave the city and had just moved its refrigeration operation to Mansfield, Ohio, eliminating 1,200 jobs. As a result, people in the city began to realize that loss of jobs in one city industry no longer meant

reemployment in another. In 1957 interest was first voiced in an industrial park in East Springfield, using land occupied by the Cottage Street Dump, the Bradley Swamp, and the Memorial Golf Course built in 1930. The site was a good location because it was near the Massachusetts Turnpike and a railroad line, and was in the midst of land already zoned for industry. Many city residents—citizens, politicians, and veterans' groups—though mindful of the city's need for job-producing industry, were unhappy with the proposal. Veterans opposed the loss of the Memorial Golf Course because it was a memorial to soldiers killed in America's wars. Others were concerned about a business "give-away," and many were suspicious of the very concept of industrial parks. The debate raged for five years, from 1956 to 1960. To satisfy critics the Memorial Golf Course was relocated to Sixteen Acres, the cost borne by the developers of the new industrial park. In 1960 ground was broken for Springfield's first industrial park, the Memorial Industrial Park. As of 1973 the park was filled, housing more than twenty-nine businesses, which employed more than 3,000 people.

Today Springfield has four industrial parks: Memorial Industrial Park on Roosevelt Avenue; Progress Industrial Park and Industry East, both off Cottage Street; and Pynchon Food Center on West Street in the North End. These parks, though not providing the thousands of industrial and manufacturing jobs once commonly available in the city, have helped Springfield maintain a dollar-generating industrial base and have provided space for new industrial construction, guaranteeing the continued existence of a number of firms within the city's limits.

Springfield is presently developing new industrial sites at Winchester Square; the Chicopee-Springfield Rifle Range Industrial Park near Interstate 291; and the North Centre Industrial Park near downtown Springfield, bounded by Dwight, Worthington, Armory, and Liberty streets, and the North End Industrial Park in the area of the Bosch plant. The first site is critical to the revitalization of the Winchester

George F. Flagg and Franck Oliver posed for this photograph after haying in the Thompson Street meadow in 1910. The area, between Bay Street and State Street, is now filled with post-World War I housing. Courtesy of George A. Flagg

Square neighborhood. The second would make use of an abandoned National Guard rifle range on the Springfield-Chicopee line. The third site will allow industry presently in the area to expand, upgrade a blighted area, allow new industry to relocate, provide jobs, and increase the city's tax base, essentially the goals of all city industrial parks. The last site is a cooperative venture between the city and the North End community to clear a blighted area and provide neighborhood people with jobs.

In September 1967 Springfield Technical Community College opened on the grounds of the Springfield Armory. The college exists to supply local business and industry with skilled labor, supplanting a function once performed by local business and industry. The college offers programs in electronics, general engineering, machinery, and medicine, replenishing the area's skilled labor supply and linking area business and industry to specific college programs. The presence of a technical college provides the skilled labor which encourages business to expand and new businesses to relocate in the Springfield area. The Massachusetts Career Development Institute, located in Springfield since 1971, has augmented the programs of Springfield Technical Community College. The skills center matches unemployed people with companies having job openings and trains them to fill available positions in electronics, the machine trades, food preparation, graphics, and electrical work.

In 1959 Springfield received a federal grant of more than 3 million dollars to begin the urban renewal of the North End in the area bounded by the arch on the south to Memorial Square on the north, Columbus Avenue to the west, and Chestnut Street to the east. Derelict buildings were cleared, allowing for the development of modern, one-story, wide buildings with room for expansion and parking lots. The section north of the arch became a location for light industry, offices, and housing: the Skyline Inn, IBM, the Liberty Medical Association building, the Standard Photo Service building, the YMCA, Chestnut Park for elderly

housing, and the Springfield Newspapers Building. Urban renewal, though it transformed a slum district, was a bittersweet experience for the city. It took almost twenty years to rebuild on cleared land, a process which still continues; and the relocation of people from the renewed section and the routing of Interstate 91 through the North End resulted in the shift of the area's population to the Winchester Square section, the center of the city's black community. A course of urban decay similar to that which occurred in the North End, racial friction, and the migration of wealthier residents, commerce, and industry to the suburbs has turned Winchester Square into an economic disaster area, offering little employment and few commercial services to the area's residents.

Basically positive and successful, the process of renewal continues in the city. The emphasis is, however, on restoration and renovation, not demolition. Springfield presently has six historical districts—Mattoon Street, McKnight, Forest Park Heights, Lower Maple, Ridgewood, and Maple Hill. The establishment of historical districts has led to the upgrading of nineteenth-century housing stock, both stabilizing and increasing property values. The city has also actively sought to revitalize in five commercial districts—downtown, the Forest Park "X," Memorial Square, the North End commercial area, and the Main Street business center of Indian Orchard—where the buildings are old and business people need help to refurbish or expand. In these areas businesses are eligible for tax-exempt bonds and Small Business Administration aid.

In response to the problems created by the rapid expansion of Sixteen Acres, the city in 1958 required that all future subdevelopments contain sanitary and storm sewers, and permanently paved streets at the expense of developers. In 1961 the city began to put in sewers and blacktop roads in the vicinity of the Memorial Golf Course.

Perhaps the most obvious signs of renewed vitality can be seen in downtown Springfield. Today the section exhibits

William Stibbs and Minnie Flagg Stibbs prepare for a trip in their Springfield-made Knox automobile, 1911. Courtesy of George A. Flagg

more building starts, renovations, and expansions than it has since the 1890s. Redevelopment, however, began slowly, lacking continued effort from the business community and supporting optimism from the city's population. In the late 1960s and early 1970s, Bay State West, a mail-hotel complex; the Civic Center, the Civic Center Garage, and the Hall of Justice were constructed. Although these buildings were part of the most ambitious building program in more than fifty years, their construction did not spark ongoing resurgence. Bay State West, built by Massachusetts Mutual to make downtown competitive with suburban malls, accelerated the decline of street-level business by drawing customers into the mall, creating more empty storefronts on Main Street.

Today downtown revitalization continues at a pace much faster than that of five or ten years ago. Today the success of downtown resurgence is due to three very closely related factors either in their infancy ten years ago or not present at that time: the gradual reappearance of a middle-class core city population, available financing for renovation or new construction, and a newly resurgent optimism concerning downtown's future. The revitalization of nineteenth-century row houses on Union and Mattoon streets has spurred the rehabilitation of other nineteenth- or early-twentieth-century structures in the downtown area. The Springfield Institution for Savings rebuilt fourteen burned-out apartments in the Spring Street area, creating the new Armoury Commons. The same bank has also converted the old Milton Bradley plant on Stockbridge Street into loft apartments. Blocks between Worthington and Lyman streets have been converted into a shopping center-apartment complex called Morgan Square. Generally, the people who are moving to the downtown neighborhood continue to create a growing need for more housing and commercial services in the area. Downtown now houses over 5,000 people and employs over 17,000.

The presence of a growing population and a growing perception that downtown renovation will be successful has spurred investment. The Marriott Hotel, part of the Bay State West complex, has added a ballroom to its facilities, and Bay State West, has undergone renovation. The northeast corner of Main Street and Harrison Avenue, vacant for ten years, was being developed by the Springfield Institution for Savings. The new Center Square, the bank's main office, includes a twelve-story office building and a two-level mall. The northwest corner of Main Street and West Court Street is the site of the Bank of Boston building, a seventeen-story office building. The trends in downtown redevelopment reflect the changed nature of the city's economy. The present economy is much less industrial and more service-oriented, staffed with white-collar workers. Since 1960, banks, specialty stores, government offices, insurance company offices, and lawyers' and doctors' offices have become increasingly common in downtown Springfield, stimulating the present development of more office, store, or housing space for the further expansion of the service industries.

The remarkable in-process revitalization of downtown is a product of public-private sector cooperation, a combination of city planning and the work of Springfield Central, an organization of downtown interests created in 1976 to draw developers and to coordinate with the city the funding of revitalization or new construction. The partnership has been successful to the extent of generating $250 million in public and private sector investments in more than 40 projects with more in the planning stage. A good example of public-private sector cooperation is the Monarch Place project now under construction. It will consist of a 26-story office tower, a 279-room Sheraton Tara hotel, and 20,000 square feet of retail space—all at a cost of $120 million. Monarch Life Insurance Company will move into the officer tower; Massachusetts Mutual Life Insurance Company will purchase Monarch's current office building to use in its own business expansion. The state and the city are providing some funds ($1.3 million); an Urban Development Action Grant will provide $10 million and Monarch will provide the rest. The

Rose Dumoszewicz Skarzynski was twenty years old when this picture was taken in 1915. Courtesy of Stanislaus J. Skarzynski

end result is that two major city employers will both expand within the city, creating more job opportunities and creating 2,300 jobs downtown—stimulating even more city economic development. Downtown must continue to be revitalized because it is the governmental, financial, commercial, and community center of the city. Money invested successfully in downtown revitalization helps to create a positive financial image for the city and will draw further investment citywide. Springfield's nineteenth-century vitality was based on a thriving economy born of investment. Downtown revitalization will help to put a similar process in operation for the next century.

Rose Dumoszewicz married Waclaw
Skarzynski, pictured here in 1930.
Together they raised a family which still
lives in the Springfield area, grandson
Stanislaus among them. Courtesy of
Stanislaus J. Skarzynski

Two views of the land in the vicinity of
North Branch Brook in Sixteen Acres in
1910. The area of Sixteen Acres was little
developed apart from farms and had
relatively unchanged natural features—
bogs, ponds, and sand flats. Courtesy of
Springfield City Library

Begun as a mill town within the city, Indian Orchard has been viewed by many as a separate community. This picture shows the mills along the Chicopee River and, barely visible, the now filled-in Indian Orchard Canal. The canal once provided power to the waterwheels of the village's mills. The picture dates from about 1880. Courtesy of Springfield City Library

The Mascot was one of four excursion boats used to transport picnickers to a privately owned, pine-shaded picnic grove now known as Riverside Park. The trip from a dock at the foot of Elm Street took thirty-five minutes. Boats such as the Mascot were in operation from the 1880s until about 1915. The growing popularity of the automobile put them out of business. Courtesy of Springfield City Library

This is Saint James Circle in July 1924. Courtesy of Springfield City Library

Established in Boston in 1870, the Chapman Valve Company moved to Indian Orchard in 1874 and began to produce gas, water, steam, and molasses valves in sixty-four patterns. The plant consisted of iron, steel, and brass foundries, machine shops, and engineering and research departments on thirty-five acres of land. During World War II the company held a large number of navy contracts for valves of all sizes, valves especially necessary in navy battleships. Courtesy of Springfield City Library

Hendee Manufacturing Co.

Renamed Indian Motocycle in 1923, the Hendee Manufacturing Company began operations in 1901 and closed in the early 1950s. At its peak Hendee employed 3,000 people. The company was the first to manufacture gasoline engine "motocycles." The R was omitted to individualize the company trademark. Especially during the early twentieth century, Indian won a number of prizes for the construction, speed, and endurance of its machines, and it supplied thirty-eight state police forces and 2,000 city, town, and county departments with motorcycles. Though about half demolished and empty, the Indian buildings are slated to be renovated for commercial use and housing by Joel Rahn. Courtesy of Springfield City Library

This is an early Indian bike circa 1907. Courtesy of Springfield City Library

This car was built in 1907 by the Atlas Motor Car Company located on Birnie Avenue. The company, one of several here in the early twentieth century, produced about 1,000 cars a year. A second car producer, the Knox Company, made motor-powered fire equipment at its plant on Wilbraham Road near Winchester Square. Courtesy of Springfield City Library

Charles E. Duryea and brother J. Frank Duryea are credited with building the first successful motor-driven car in 1892. The Duryea Motor Car Company was founded in 1895, and the first models sold for between $1,000 and $2,000. In this 1898 picture four fireman pose in an early Duryea in front of the Winchester Square Fire Station. The car belonged to the fire chief and was called his "hurry-up-run-about." Courtesy of Springfield City Library

Founded in 1910, American Bosch, now a division of Limited Technologies located at the northern end of Brightwood, began operation as a manufacturer of magnetos used on early automobile ignition systems. Today the complex produces automobile parts. Courtesy of Springfield City Library

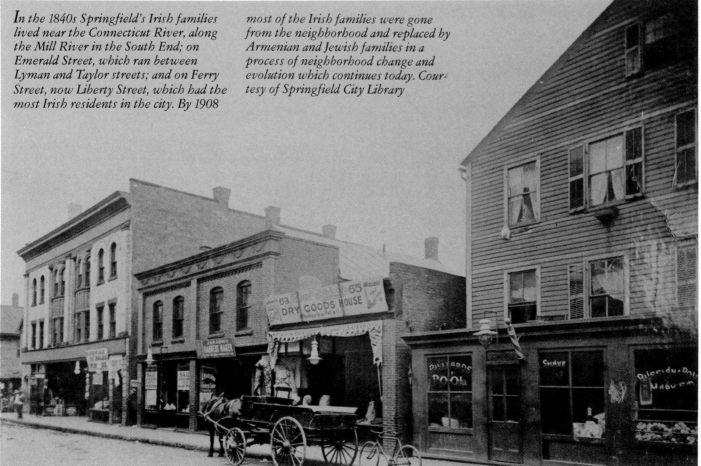

In the 1840s Springfield's Irish families lived near the Connecticut River, along the Mill River in the South End; on Emerald Street, which ran between Lyman and Taylor streets; and on Ferry Street, now Liberty Street, which had the most Irish residents in the city. By 1908 most of the Irish families were gone from the neighborhood and replaced by Armenian and Jewish families in a process of neighborhood change and evolution which continues today. Courtesy of Springfield City Library

In 1906 Albert Steiger opened a department store on the north corner of Main and Hillman streets. By the late 1920s, company expansion filled the entire block from Hillman Street north to Bridge Street. The three-story bay window fronting Steiger's on Main Street is the renovated Orr block, which was built in 1883 and incorporated into the department store's twentieth-century construction. The picture dates from the 1880s. Courtesy of Springfield City Library

Massachusetts Mutual built this eight-story building in 1907-08 on the southwest corner of State and Main streets. At 123 feet, it was the tallest building in the city apart from churches with spires. After it was built, Springfield pressed the state legislature for a 125-foot maximum height for buildings in the city. This limitation held until Bay State West was built. By the late 1920s this building had become too small for business, and the insurance company moved to its present site on upper State Street. Courtesy of John Polak

This is a view of Main Street in 1914. Courtesy of Springfield City Library

An early twentieth-century view of Main Street from the railroad arch shows the Massasoit House on the right; the mixed transportation of the early century, house, auto, or electric trolley; and the marquee for the Nelson Theatre advertising "advanced" vaudeville. Courtesy of Springfield City Library

This is Doris Mansfield of Bay Street as she appeared in 1918. Courtesy of George A. Flagg

Walter Rosenberg is shown on his thirteenth birthday and bar mitzvah, on September 11, 1915. He became a bandleader in the 1930s and 1940s. Courtesy of Frank H. Freedman

The Springfield City Library on State Street was completed in 1912. Andrew Carnegie, impressed by the city's civic spirit and development, donated $200,000 towards the cost of construc- tion. Local gifts raised an additional $150,000. This building replaced the old city library (1876) which stood at about the same location. Courtesy of Stanis- laus J. Skarzynski

This view of the Worthy Hotel, built in 1895 and located on the southeast corner of Main and Worthington streets, was taken in 1911-12. At that time the Worthy now renovated as housing for the elderly, was one of the best-known hotels in the city. Courtesy of Springfield City Library

The Municipal Group, dedicated in 1913, replaced the old city hall (1854) which burned in 1905. The group, located on West Court Street, is a blending of Greek and Roman architectural styles. The old city hall, according to tradition, burned when a kerosene lamp was knocked over by a monkey while a fair was being held in the building's large exhibition hall. The old city hall bell, which crashed to the ground during the fire, is now a planter in front of the present city hall. Courtesy of Stanislaus J. Skarzynski

In 1911 a member of the Industrial Workers of the World, a radical labor organization, planted a bomb in the then-under-construction Municipal Tower. Little damage was done, and the bomber was arrested, convicted, and sent to prison. Sketch by Robert Holcomb; courtesy of Springfield City Library

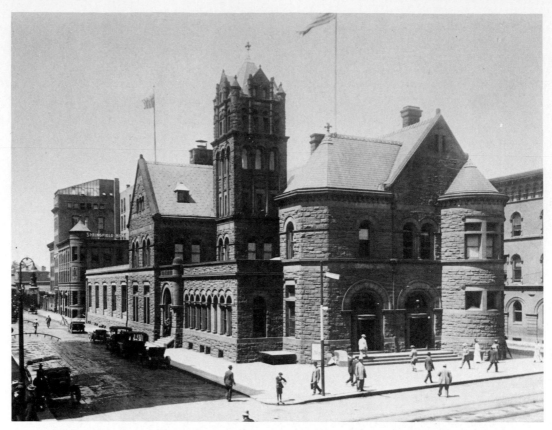

This is a 1914 depiction of the Springfield Post Office and Customs House, built in 1889. It stood on the northwest corner of Main and Worthington streets until 1931. Courtesy of Springfield City Library

The Springfield Street Railway Company began operating horse-drawn trolleys in 1870, with stables at Main and Hooker streets. The first track was almost three miles long and ran from Hooker Street along Main Street to the intersection of State, then up State Street to Oak Street. In 1910 the system, electrified in 1890, had (including the suburbs) 137 miles of track. The company then owned 389 cars and carried almost 24 million passengers a year. The company ceased to exist in November 1981. Here workmen repair a section of roadbed. Courtesy of Springfield City Library

The alligator pool at Forest Park in 1910 was one of a wide variety of live animal exhibits. By the mid-1970s animal exhibits, except for a small, privately-operated zoo and a city-maintained aviary, were discontinued. High maintenance costs, as well as the decay and obsolescence of zoo buildings, cages, and equipment, made closing of the exhibits necessary. The aviary is now gone. Courtesy of Springfield City Library

Paternal great-grandfather of Kelley J. Talbot, Phillippe Guertin (1888-1968), poses in his uniform of the Catholic Order of Forresters, about 1910. Courtesy of Kelley J. Talbot

Pecousic Villa, demolished in 1959 for relocation of Route 5, was built in 1883 by Everett H. Barney and was his home until he died in 1916. The contractor, John Lizak of Palmer, Massachusetts, offered to pay the city ten dollars to tear down the building. Other companies wanted $1,000 or more to do the job. The city accepted the ten-dollar offer, and the contractor carefully removed hand-painted Italian tiles; Belgian bronze work around the fireplaces; stained-glass windows; cherrywood, oak, and mahogany paneling; and exotic European, Egyptian, Chinese, and Indian trees and shrubs from the grounds. Courtesy of Springfield City Library

The Barney estate in 1890 was maintained by an army of gardeners. Courtesy of Springfield City Library

This is a view of Main Street in 1914. Courtesy of Springfield City Library

Market Street in 1914 was the location of the Central Labor Union Hall. The hall housed an alliance of area labor unions seeking to improve working conditions for their members and to find jobs for the unemployed. In the early nineteenth century, Market Street was the place where unemployed men gathered. Employers went there and hired from this informally organized manpower pool. Courtesy of Springfield City Library

The Charles McKnight house on Riverview Terrace is typical of early twentieth-century rejection of Victorian styling. The design is clearly geometrical, and ornamentation is limited. Courtesy of John Polak

During World War I, women replaced many men in American factories. Women knitted sweaters and socks for soldiers, supported bond drives, and maintained vegetable gardens in order to add to the nation's food supply. Here women work at the armory. The picture dates from 1918. Courtesy of Springfield City Library

These unusual twin bungalows of one-story construction and gently pitched, gabled roofs were built on the west corner of Lakeside Avenue and Alden Street in 1914-15. Courtesy of John Polak

During the nineteen months of World War I, the Springfield Armory produced more than 250,000 1903 Springfield rifles, "the most acclaimed military firearm in history," according to General George Patton. Courtesy of Springfield City Library

This World War I parade and rally was made up of women working at the armory. Courtesy of Springfield Armory National Historic Site Archives

This is a Springfield Armory machine gun class during World War I. Courtesy of Springfield Armory National Historic Site Archives

The 104th Regiment of the Twenty-sixth Yankee Division returns to Springfield and the Howard Street National Guard Armory at the end of World War I in 1918. Courtesy of Springfield City Library

George S. L. Connor presents a framed scroll to former mayor Daniel G. Brunton in 1958. Connor was chaplain for the 104th Infantry, Twenty-sixth Yankee Division, during World War I. He helped the wounded and consoled the dying. He was once pastor of Holy Name Church in the Forest Park neighborhood. Courtesy of Springfield City Library

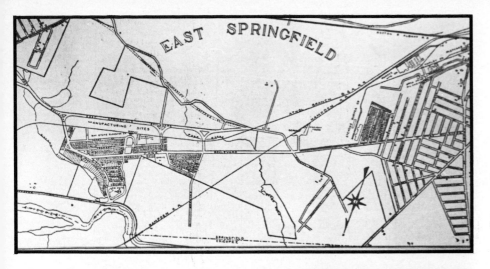

Except for in-place or planned industrial development along Page Boulevard and Saint James Avenue, little residential development had occurred in East Springfield as of 1915. Courtesy of Springfield City Library

This is a view of State Street, July 1924. Courtesy of Springfield City Library

These unidentified children were photographed playing at Emily Bill Playground on Franklin Street in 1920. Nathan D. Bill (1855-1947), city businessman and philanthropist, donated five playgrounds to the city of Springfield so that children would not have to play in the streets. He named this park after his mother. Bill also aided in the development of the city's golf courses. He is an excellent example of the nineteenth-century business ethic that a prosperous businessman should return to his community some of the business profits he made in that community. Courtesy of Springfield City Library

An Americanization class for immigrants posed at the Boston and Albany Railroad shops in 1929. Only the teachers are identified: center left, Mrs. Agnes B. Egan; and center right, Mrs. Margaret Bresnan. Courtesy of Springfield City Library

Radasch Incorporated, "haberdasher and men's outfitter," was one of many downtown retail clothiers operating at a number of locations for almost fifty years. Courtesy of Springfield City Library

This is a Kibbe advertising stamp dating from circa 1920. Courtesy of Springfield City Library

Johanna Bieniewicz, in pictures dating from the early 1920s, models clothes designed and handmade by her mother, Ceslawa. The shoes modeled in these pictures were bought in Meekins, Packard and Wheat, a once-prominent downtown department store which closed during the Depression. The hats were made by Levison's, famous in the 1920s for handmade hats. Courtesy of Mrs. Joseph Bieniewicz Brusnicki

Joseph B. Brusnicki, pictured here in 1921, came to Springfield in 1905. Mr. Brusnicki was a prominent pharmacist in Springfield for fifty years, serving as president of both the Massachusetts Pharmaceutical Association and the Springfield Druggist Association. Courtesy of Joseph B. Brusnicki

This photo shows Allen Street at Cooley Street, May 1924. Courtesy of Springfield City Library

This is a view of Cooley Street, August 1924. Courtesy of Springfield City Library

During the 1920s Springfield police tried to enforce Prohibition, the Eighteenth Amendment, by raiding stills and speakeasies and dumping illegal liquor down sewers and into the Connecticut River. City neighborhoods never lacked bathtub gin, and the South End always had wine. Sketch by Robert Holcomb; courtesy of Springfield City Library

In 1924 the intersection of Sumner Avenue and Allen Street had not lost its rural appearance. Before 1860 Allen Street, named for the Allen family, was known as South Wilbraham or Hampden Road. Courtesy of Springfield City Library

In the 1920s Middlesex Street, running south of Wilbraham Road and named for Middlesex County in Massachusetts, was little more than a dirt path. Courtesy of Springfield City Library

The Richardson-designed railroad station was replaced in 1926 by the present Union Station, which was sold to a private developer in 1970. Except for a small portion of the station renovated and used by Amtrak, the building is empty. Courtesy of Springfield City Library

Edwin S. Gardner was a prominent city lawyer and owner of the Court Square Theater. Gardner built this Jacobean revival home on Maple Street in 1928. Courtesy of John Polak

The Harold G. Duckworth house, built in 1931 on Longhill Street, is noted for its gables, slate roofs, chimneys, half-timbering, and brick and stone work. Members of the Duckworth family founded and managed the present-day Rexnord plant in the Memorial Industrial Park. Courtesy of John Polak

Between 1934, when this picture was taken, and 1940, buses replaced trolleys on the streets of the city. Courtesy of Springfield City Library

Between the years 1929 and 1939, Springfield was in the midst of the Great Depression, suffering unemployment and poverty. The result was Roosevelt's New Deal and such projects as the rebuilding of North Branch Parkway, designed to improve city roads and give people work. Courtesy of Springfield City Library

The city dump on Wilbraham Road was the site of the O'Shay Hotel in the early 1930s. During the winter hot meals were provided for men working on various federal projects. The meals cost eight to ten cents apiece for men paid $2.50 a day for their labor. Entertainment was provided by out-of-work musicians. Courtesy of Springfield City Library

On March 11, 1936, Springfield experienced a rainstorm which dropped up to three inches of rain on the city. This and thawing temperatures led to the worst flood in city history. Dikes burst in the North End, and 8,000 people left for higher ground. One thousand homes were abandoned in the South End. Nineteenth- and twentieth-century flooding in Springfield led to the development of the city's housing problems. Many buildings, damaged as a result of flooding and never properly refurbished or repaired, became substandard housing stock in the North and South ends. The view is of Columbus Avenue looking south. Courtesy of Springfield City Library

On September 21, 1938, after days of rain, a hurricane swept down the Connecticut Valley. Without warning, 100-mile-per-hour winds swept into Springfield, smashing the Goodyear blimp at Springfield Airport, blowing over trees, and creating whitecaps on the Connecticut River, which lashed at the river bridges. Ten thousand people were evacuated from the North and South ends. The view is of South Main Street looking north. Courtesy of Springfield City Library

SHOW BOAT PRINCIPALS

Springfield Spiritual Singers
Edwin Clark --Joe
Center in Group who sings
"Old Man River"

The Springfield Spiritual Singers featuring Edwin Clark, center, were featured in a Kiwanis Club program in 1932. Courtesy of Springfield City Library

During the 1930s the Grenville brothers designed and built the Gee Bee, named after the Grenville Brothers. Nicknamed the "flying piano stool" because of its unusual design, the plane won a number of air races. Some of the design features, such as a single control stick, were incorporated into American World War II fighter aircraft. A number of models were built at and flew out of the Springfield Airport, now a shopping plaza in East Springfield. Courtesy of Springfield City Library

Eleanor Powell of Springfield, described as the Pavlova of tap dancing, was under contract with Hollywood movie makers and was working on the New York stage when this picture was taken in 1935. Courtesy of Springfield City Library

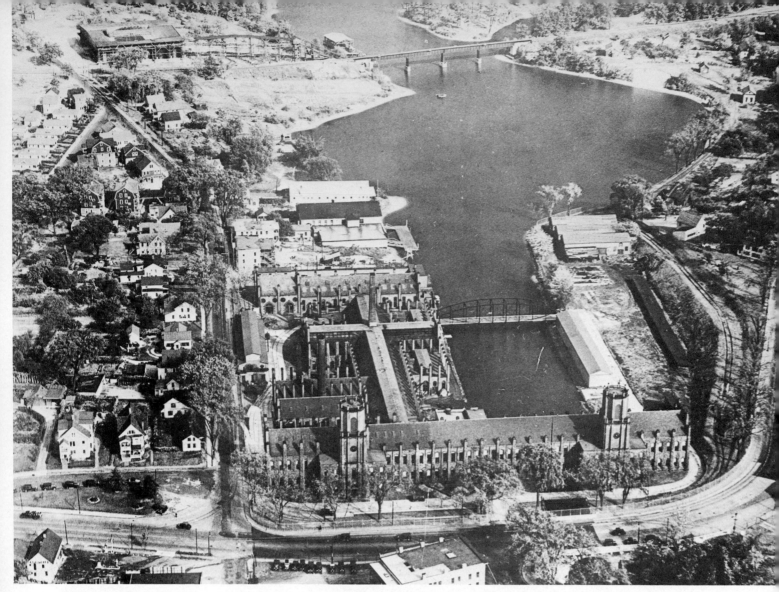

This is a view of the Armory watershops complex as it appeared in the 1930s. Here rifle parts were finished. Courtesy of Springfield Armory National Historic Site Archives

Springfield Safe Deposit and Trust Company, now Shawmut First Bank and Trust Company, was built in 1932 in Art Deco style with a linear, geometric facade and stylized decoration. Courtesy of Stanislaus J. Skarzynski

This is a view of Main Street, June 1940, looking north. To the right is Liggett's Drug Store, now the location of Mall Drug. The Moorish arches of the old Fuller Block, now the Forum Building, remain unchanged from their original construction of 1889. Courtesy of Springfield City Library

Roger L. Putnam, center right, was a three-term mayor of Springfield, from 1937 through 1943. During World War II Putnam was director of research and development of the Amphibious Force of the Atlantic Fleet and participated in the Normandy invasion, receiving a commendation. Putnam convinced the city to build a trade school in 1938, now the Roger L. Putnam Vocational Technical High School. Courtesy of Springfield City Library

Henry J. Gamble served in the U.S. Navy during World War II, with the navy postal service in New York City. After the war he was employed by the United States Post Office, retiring in 1966. Courtesy of Mrs. Marilyn Gamble Gourinski

Benny Goodman and his Spotlite Band appear at a World War II band rally at the Springfield Armory in 1944. Courtesy of Springfield Armory National Historic Site Archives

Again looking north from the intersection of State and Main streets, one can see a second view of Main Street in June 1940. Today the Civic Center is on the right. Up the street on the left, the light-colored building, once a nineteenth-century tavern, is the site of the Bank of Boston building. Courtesy of Springfield City Library

Sophie Przekop, twenty-one years old, finishes a rifle stock at the Springfield Armory in 1943. Women successfully filled jobs left vacant as men joined the military for war duty. Courtesy of Springfield Armory National Historical Site Archives

In 1943 Charles H. Hills ground rifle barrels at the Springfield Armory. Courtesy of Springfield Armory National Historic Site Archives

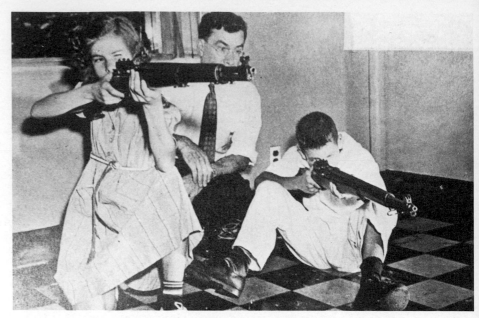

John C. Garand, a native of Canada, began working at the Springfield Armory in 1919. In that year he began to develop a self-loading rifle. In 1936 the armed forces of the United States adopted the M-1 rifle. In 1940 the armory went into twenty-four-hour-a-day operation, producing 5 million M-1s during World War II. General Patton considered the M-1 the "greatest weapon ever made." Here Garand's children demonstrate their target-shooting ability with the M-1. Courtesy of Springfield City Library

This is a World War II Army Signal Corps sergeant carrying a Springfield-designed and produced M-1 Garand rifle in 1943. Courtesy of Springfield Armory National Historic Site Archives

Army Lieutenant Colonel Douglas B. Wesson, 1884-1956, was vice-president of Smith and Wesson Company, 1920-1940. He served in the tank corps during World War I and returned to active duty in 1940, serving in an ordnance unit during World War II. Courtesy of Springfield City Library

The Bay State Thread Company began producing uniform cloth for the Union army in a Mill River building. During World War II, the company, a subcontractor, supplied thread used in stitching different types of military equipment such as parachutes, boots, cartridge belts, and helmets. Mr. C. E. Chaffin, president of the firm, is seen inspecting the equipment. Courtesy of Springfield City Library

Now part of Easco Corporation of Maryland, the Moore Corporation, originally organized to drop-forge metal bicycle parts, did all kinds of forging during World War II, from tank parts to surgical equipment. The company, located at the old Wason Railway Car Company works in Brightwood, is a principal supplier of wrenches to Sears. Courtesy of Springfield City Library

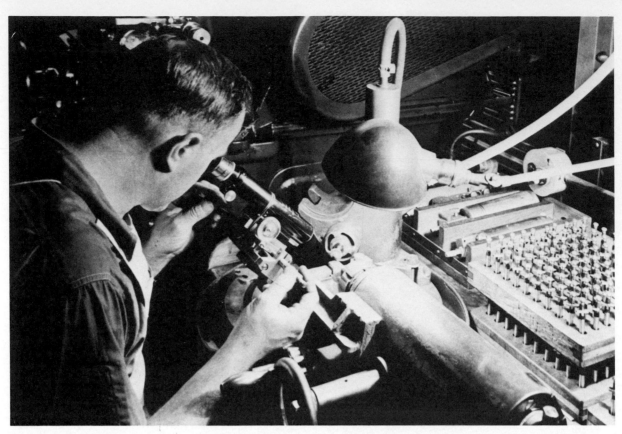

By 1940 American Bosch, now a division of United Technologies, was the leading American manufacturer of fuel injection equipment used on diesel engines. The company also produced magnetos used on American aircraft during World War II, and employed 1,500 people in 1940. *Courtesy of Springfield City Library*

This is a photograph of Master Sergeant Sanford Rosenberg, right, and Ensign Frank H. Freedman in 1945. Ensign Freedman became mayor of Springfield and is today a federal judge. *Courtesy of Frank H. Freedman*

In the summer of 1942, Cecil L. Denis of East Springfield was in basic training at Camp Polk, Louisiana. He is holding a 1903 Springfield rifle and wearing a World War I shallow helmet and puttees—standard army equipment in 1942. *Courtesy of John Denis*

An unidentified Springfield girl poses in front of a World War II bond drive poster. From the author's collection

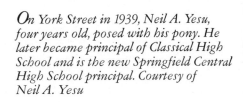

On York Street in 1939, Neil A. Yesu, four years old, posed with his pony. He later became principal of Classical High School and is the new Springfield Central High School principal. Courtesy of Neil A. Yesu

181

Once located on Taylor Street and later on Liberty, the Cheney Bigelow Wire Works was founded in 1842, producing a wide range of wire products. During World War II the company developed an anti-tank bazooka used successfully in that war and in Korea. The company closed in the 1970s. Courtesy of Springfield City Library

INTERIORS, CHENEY BIGELOW WIRE WORKS.

Mrs. Elly Matz carried her son Arnold out of the Soviet Union at the end of World War II, evading both the retreating German army and the advancing Russian army. Courtesy of Arnold Matz

A view of Carew Street hill taken in 1946 shows the old Mercy Hospital buildings. Courtesy of Springfield City Library

Looking southeast in the area of Blunt Park one can see the Saint James Avenue dry bridge near the Tapley Street intersection. Courtesy of Springfield City Library

Anthony W. D'Agostino and Lucy D'Agostino Fitzgerald, brother and sister, posed for this picture on Easter Sunday 1946 on Adam Street. Courtesy of Traci D'Agostino

Oliver Petell poses on his three-wheeler on a South End corner in 1946. Mr. Petell is now a printer in Springfield. Courtesy of Carol P. Petell

In 1946 the Island Pond area between Roosevelt Avenue and Plumtree Road was referred to as a new community, since it was being developed so rapidly. Courtesy of Springfield City Library

The Glenwood neighborhood just above the present-day Bay State Medical Center shows the edge of Van Horn Park to the right. The white spot in the upper right corner was Springfield Airport, now Springfield Plaza shopping center. Courtesy of Springfield City Library

This view of Indian Orchard shows the Chicopee River and Ludlow beyond. The picture dates from 1946. Courtesy of Springfield City Library

Photographed in 1954, the Italian Feast at Mount Carmel Church on William Street featured a greased pole climb, a variety of Italian foods and entertainment, and this procession during which a statue of Our Lady of Mount Carmel is carried through the streets of the South End. Courtesy of Lori J. Perez

This is a 1951 view of the intersection of Sanford and Main streets, the present site of the Civic Center. Courtesy of Springfield City Library

The intersection of Broadway and Vernon as it appeared in 1951 no longer exists. Today Bay State West occupies the upper right-hand corner of the picture, and Route 91 and East and West Columbus Avenue occupy the left side. Courtesy of Springfield City Library

A 1951 view of Winchester Square shows it at the height of its vitality. The picture was taken from the roof of the apartment block next to Shiloh Church. The buildings on the left side of the picture have since been demolished, leaving open space. Courtesy of Springfield City Library

Thomas J. O'Connor, now a Hampden County commissioner, was the youngest mayor in the history of Springfield when first elected in 1957 at the age of thirty-two. He served three terms as mayor. O'Connor was instrumental in the early revitalization of the city, especially in the establishment of off-street parking and stricter regulations requiring developers to install storm drains and pave the streets of new city subdivisions. Courtesy of Springfield City Library

Anthony M. Scibelli has served Springfield in the Massachusetts House of Representatives since 1960. He was instrumental in the establishment of Springfield Technical Community College on the grounds of the now defunct Springfield Armory. Courtesy of Springfield Public Library

Two views of slum conditions in the area of lower Carew Street in Springfield in the 1950s show the degree to which nineteenth-century housing stock had deteriorated. Buildings which were quaint or charming in pictures dating from the 1890s were, by the 1950s, in desperate need of renovation or demolition. Courtesy of Springfield City Library

This view of the intersection of State and Main streets in 1964 shows Northeast Savings in construction, and a parking lot where the Civic Center stands today. Courtesy of Springfield City Library

These three views of the North End urban renewal area taken in 1967 from the Holiday Inn show the extent of demolition. The first picture shows Ferry and Liberty streets; the second, the remains of lower Franklin Street; and the third, the Technicolor Building and the then-rising post office building. Courtesy of Springfield City Library

*B*etween 1967 and 1972, the Holiday Inn (extreme left), the IBM Building (right corner), a state office building, and a new YMCA were constructed in the city's New North, the old North End. In this 1972 view, the Technicolor Studios buildings rise right of the center of the picture. Left of center is the Standard Photo Building. Courtesy of Springfield City Library

*T*he Springfield Newspaper Building, constructed in 1972, occupies a city block across the street from the United States Postal Service and Federal Building. In the background are Interstates 91 and 291, completed about 1970. Courtesy of Springfield City Library

Dr. Frederick F. Driftmier was pastor of Springfield's South Congregational Church for twenty-four years, from 1955 to 1979. He served as an educator, a public speaker, and a member of numerous boards and agencies. Courtesy of Springfield City Library

James L. Grimaldi, active in politics for more than twenty-five years, served on the City Council as well as in the State House of Representatives. Throughout his career Grimaldi was especially interested in the revitalization of Main Street as well as in mass transportation in the Springfield area and statewide. Courtesy of Springfield City Library

Leonard A. Corbin was appointed Springfield's first black fireman in 1969. Courtesy of Springfield City Library

The Springfield Armory closed in April 1968. The armory was the industrial heart of a once-industrial city. Today the grounds are occupied by a national park, Springfield Technical Community College, and industry. The closing ceremony took place in front of the main arsenal building of the old armory, constructed between 1847 and 1852. The armory is now the center of the national park. Courtesy of Springfield City Library

During the post-World War II period, Springfield energetically and successfully sought to replace a decaying railroad system with interstate highways. The interstates were viewed as a means to develop or revitalize the city's commerce and industry. The interstates considerably altered the face of the city and the pace of city travel, and contributed to the decentralization of commerce and industry. This is a south view of the intersection of Routes 91 and 291 in 1972 in Springfield. Courtesy of Springfield City Library

Roundhill, a prominent city neighborhood in the north end and actually a hill, was completely eliminated by the construction of Route 91. Martha Blackstone, daughter of a prominent family and a Springfield teacher, was murdered here by a gun-toting second-story man in 1910. Tradition says that the murder, deeply shocking to the community, marked the beginning of door-locking in Springfield. Courtesy of Springfield City Library

Thaddeus J. Brusnicki, production engineer, Armory Ordnance Division, Springfield Armory, helped design the M-14 rifle for the armory. Courtesy of Springfield Armory National Historic Site Archives

Developed between 1890 and 1910, the McKnight section contained the city's largest houses. By 1940 Springfield's well-to-do began to leave for the suburbs; between 1930 and 1940, assessed values had dropped by one-quarter, and conversion to multi-family dwellings began. Conversion was seen in 1940 as a neighborhood salvation but actually spurred neighborhood decay. Today the McKnight section is a historical district and multi-family conversion is forbidden. Shown here is Dartmouth Street in 1892. Courtesy of Springfield City Library

In 1960 the Memorial Golf Course on Roosevelt Avenue was purchased and, by 1962, about 350 acres of land were made available for industrial sites. Memorial Industrial Park's first tenant, the Springfield Gas Light Company, now Bay State Gas Company, opened in the spring of 1964. Courtesy of Springfield City Library

The Springfield Civic Center opened in 1972. With a 10,000-seat arena as well as banquet and conference rooms, the civic center contributes to city revitalization as an entertainment-convention center. Courtesy of Stanislaus J. Skarzynski

Completed in 1982 the Federal Building is on Main Street north of Bay State West. It is a six-story structure located on the southwest corner of Main and Worthington streets. The building, with a glass-enclosed multi-story atrium, consolidates thirteen federal agencies employing about 360 people. Courtesy of Springfield City Library

Judith and John Denis were active with several militia units during the nation's bicentennial celebrations, including battle reenactments and lectures. Here they wear clothing of the late eighteenth century. Courtesy of John Denis

Neri Perez came to Springfield in the early 1950s from Catalina, Puerto Rico when he was twenty-one. At that time, snow was a new experience for him. Today Mr. Perez owns and operates his own barbershop in Chicopee. Courtesy of Lori J. Perez

Lori J. Perez, plans to be an elementary school teacher. Courtesy of Lori J. Perez

Under construction here on the northeast corner of Main Street and Harrison Avenue, Center Square, opened in 1982, includes a twelve-story office tower and a two-level, glassed-in mall connected to Steiger's Department Store. The building, developed by the Spring-field Institution for Savings as the location of the bank's main office, occupies a tract of land which was cleared for development in 1972. Courtesy of Stanislaus J. Skarzynski

Paul Mason served on the City Council for many years. Active in politics for more than thirty years, Mason has been involved with many community organizations, serving on the boards of the Springfield YMCA, Junior Achievement, and the Red Cross. Courtesy of Springfield City Library

Theodore E. Dimauro, three term mayor of Springfield who left office in 1984, worked successfully with the business community to inject new life into downtown Springfield. Courtesy of Springfield City Library

196

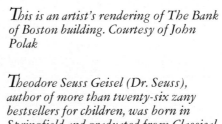

This is an artist's rendering of The Bank of Boston building. Courtesy of John Polak

Theodore Seuss Geisel (Dr. Seuss), author of more than twenty-six zany bestsellers for children, was born in Springfield and graduated from Classical High School. Here Dr. Seuss (right) and then Mayor Frank H. Freedman appear at American International College's commencement in 1970. Courtesy of Frank H. Freedman

Seventeen-year-old Doreen Conelley of Springfield was chosen Miss Springdale Mall in 1974. Courtesy of Doreen C. Pray

Alfred Conelley, Jr., and daughter, Heather, as they appeared in 1967. Mr. Conelley, a pilot in the U.S. Air Force for twenty-two years, served all over the world as well as in World War II and the Korean War. Courtesy of Alice M. Conelley

Demetria R. Greer, posed for this picture in 1981. Courtesy of Classical High School

Bay State West, containing a twenty-nine story tower, a 270-room hotel, and a two-level shopping mall, was built at a cost of $57 million by Massachusetts Mutual Life Insurance Company. Opened in 1971, it was downtown Springfield's first move in the direction of large-scale revitalization and a break with the more traditional red brick, limited-height buildings of the late nineteenth and early twentieth centuries. Courtesy of Stanislaus J. Skarzynski

Stanislaus J. Skarzynski, principal photographer for this book, is a native of Springfield. He is a Springfield Firefighter. He also does photographic work for the Journal of Massachusetts History *published by Westfield State College. Courtesy of Stanislaus J. Skarzynski*

An early 1960s view of the Municipal Group shows a skyline which has altered much in twenty years. Courtesy of Springfield City Library

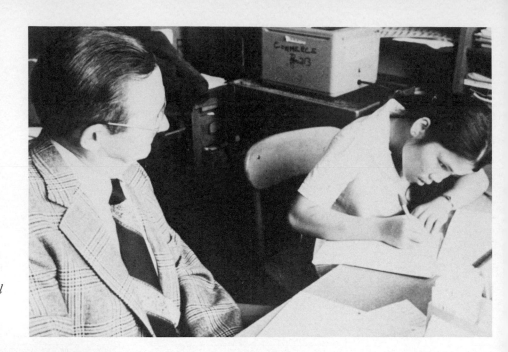

Mr. Ellis Ross, a member of DOVES (Dedicated Older Volunteers' Educational Service), tutors a student in English at Commerce High School. Courtesy of Springfield City Library

Springfield Public Schools superintendent, Thomas J. Donahoe, receives a plaque from James K. Tillotson, supervisor of social studies in Springfield. Courtesy of Springfield Public Schools

Hutson W. Inniss plays the baritone tenor horn for the Classical High School band at a football game in 1981. Courtesy of Classical High School

Mrs. Constance Tarpey, a volunteer in the Springfield Public Schools, explains pond life at Venture Pond on Wilbraham Road to a group of students from Glickman Elementary School. Courtesy of Springfield Public Schools

Eastmont Development Corporation is presently renovating the old YMCA building for market rate housing. The cost of the project is $6 million and is scheduled to be completed in 1986. It will also include a health club and attached parking. Courtesy of Springfield Central

Developed by Fontaine Brothers at a cost of $6 million and completed in 1981, Marketplace consists of rehabilitated buildings with all new interiors facing a pedestrian walkway which was once a street, Market Street. Courtesy of Springfield Central

In 1979, at a cost of $2.2 million, a vacant industrial building was rehabilitated for WGBH, Channel 57—Western Massachusetts' PBS station. A small park, typical of the increasing greenspace downtown, was also completed next to the building. Courtesy of Springfield Central

St. James Properties, with an investment of $6 million, is presently renovating the old Fuller Block. The intent of the developers is to restore the building to its original "Moorish" appearance. Courtesy of Springfield Central

Columbus Center, owned by the Springfield Parking Authority and developed by the city at a cost of $9 million, was completed in 1984. It contains the S. Prestley Blake Theater, seating almost 500, and a 150-seat capacity theater, the Winifred Arms Theater for special community programs. It is also the home of a resident theater company, Stagewest. Courtesy of Springfield Central

The Board of Trade Block on Main Street, built between 1862 and 1875, is actually three buildings. Strehlke Corpora- tion will rehabilitate it at a cost of $1.3 million. Courtesy of Springfield Central

Monarch Place, the "jewel" of downtown revitalization will be the new home of Monarch Life Insurance Company and will contain a tower with

350,000 square feet of office space, as well as a health club and a convention center. Courtesy of Hayes Associates

The old Paramount Block, once home for the Massasoit House, is scheduled for renovation by CMC Developers at an estimated cost, excluding the movie theater, of $3 million. Courtesy of Springfield Central

Built in 1896 the Terminal Block, on the northeast corner of Main and Lyman streets, and once known as the Mayflower Hotel, is scheduled for renovation by CMC Developers at a cost of $4.4 million. The wall east of the building will be beautified with cascading flowers and shrubs. Courtesy of Springfield Central

It is almost a miracle that a non-commercial early-nineteenth-century structure continues to exist in the midst of Springfield's central business district, an area noted for its high real estate values and its successive generations of structural alteration, demolition, and redevelopment. Old First Church is Springfield's most obvious architectural link with the city's three preceding centuries of history. Courtesy of Stanislaus J. Skarzynski

The game of basketball—a true American sport—was invented in Springfield in 1891 by Dr. James Naismith of Springfield College. It is only fitting, therefore, that the only national Basketball Hall of Fame be located in "Basketball City, U.S.A."—Springfield.

SELECTED BIBLIOGRAPHY

Barrows, Charles H. *The History of Springfield for the Young.* Springfield, 1911.

Bauer, Frank. *At the Crossroads: Springfield, Massachusetts, 1636-1975.* Springfield, 1975.

Brown, Richard D. *Urbanization in Springfield, Massachusetts, 1790-1830.* Springfield, 1962.

Burns, Kathryne, ed. *Springfield's Ethnic Heritage* series. 8 vols. Springfield, 1976.

Burt, Henry M. *The First Century of the History of Springfield.* 2 vols. Springfield, 1898.

Clark, James. *Springfield Streets.* 2 vols. Springfield, 1947.

Copeland, Alfred M. *Our Country and Its People: A History of Hampden County.* Massachusetts. 3 vols. Boston, 1902.

Cummings, Naomi and others. *The History of St. John's Congregational Church.* Springfield, 1962.

Frisch, Michael. *Town Into City.* Cambridge, 1972.

Green, Mason A. *Springfield Memories.* Springfield, 1876.

_____. *Springfield: 1636-1886.* Boston, 1888.

Holland, J. G. *History of Western Massachusetts.* 2 vols. Springfield, 1855.

Innes, Stephen. *Labor in a New Land.* Princeton, 1983.

Johnson, Clifton. *Hampden County, 1636-1936.* New York, 1936.

King, Moses, ed. *King's Handbook of Springfield.* Springfield, 1884.

McIntyre, Ruth A. *William Pynchon: Merchant and Colonizer.* Springfield, 1961.

Smith, Joseph H., ed. *Colonial Justice in Western Massachusetts, the Pynchon Court Records (1636-1702).* Cambridge, 1962.

Taylor, Robert J. *Western Massachusetts in the Revolution.* Providence, 1954.

Tomlinson, Juliette. *Pynchon Papers* (vol. 1). *Letters of John Pynchon 1654-1700.* Boston, 1982.

Tomlinson, Juliette, and Frances Armytage. *The Pynchons of Springfield, Founders and Colonizers, 1636-1702.* Springfield, 1959.

Whittlesey, Derwent. *The Springfield Armory: A Study in Institutional Development* (unpub. dis.). Chicago, 1920.

Wright, Harry Andrew. *The Story of Western Massachusetts* (4 vol). New York, 1949.

_____. *Papers and Proceedings of the Connecticut Valley Historical Society* (4 vols.). Springfield, 1876-1907.

_____. *Springfield Scrapbooks.* Local History Room, Springfield City Library.

_____. Vertical files. Local History Room, Springfield City Library.

INDEX

Donald J. D'Amato is a native of Springfield, Massachusetts. He received his B.A. from American International College in Springfield, and his M.A. and Ph.D. from the University of Connecticut. Dr. D'Amato is a sought-after speaker, having lectured to regional schools, clubs, and business organizations. He also appears regularly on area television and radio stations. He is a teacher at Springfield's Classical High School.